Like a Great River
AN INTRODUCTION TO HINDUISM

Like a Great River

AN INTRODUCTION TO HINDUISM

Herbert Stroup

HARPER & ROW, PUBLISHERS

New York, Evanston, San Francisco, London

To My Daughter
Trudi Ann

Nil mortalibus ardui est.
Horace, *Odes*, I, iii, 37

FIRST EDITION

STANDARD BOOK NUMBER: 06-067757-0

LIBRARY OF CONGRESS CATALOG CARD NUMBER: 72-78049

CONTENTS

Preface

This elementary book seeks to serve as an introduction to a highly complex religion: Hinduism. Admittedly on this subject countless volumes have been written. While some of them are simple in design, many are technical in character and require that the reader bring the proper tools of scholarship to their understanding. This book, however, is intended for those readers who have little or no competency in Hinduism or for the person with knowledge who wishes to review. The notable rise in the recent years of wide interest in Eastern religions, including Hinduism, calls for basically interpretative works that seek to describe in as objective terms as possible the nature of these religions.

Since this book is intended for the general reader, the apparatus of scholarship has been kept to a minimum. There are no footnotes, although the author recognizes his indebtedness to the scholarly works of others. He knows, too, that on many points presented in this book in relatively straightforward fashion there are serious disagreements among authorities in the field. At every turn he has sought merely to rest his description upon knowledge that is widely, although not universally, admitted. A brief, annotated bibliography has been included, with the hope that the beginning reader may wish to explore further some of the themes developed in this book. Purposefully, the bibliography is directed toward the person with little or no knowledge of Hinduism.

Other aids for the general reader also have been included. A glossary of technical terms used throughout the book is included within the subject index. Again, various names and terms within the Hindu tradition are spelled in English variously by different scholars. The chief virtue of their present usage is consistency. In this regard the use of diacritical marks and other signs of complete accuracy have been eliminated.

I am deeply appreciative of the critical reading of the manuscript by my respected friend, Professor Henry Clay Niles of Westminster College, Fulton, Missouri. As an authority in the history of religions his sharp eye kept me from making a number of mistakes.

Although indebted to many persons, including those mentioned above, the author must remain responsible as do all authors for the substance of his work.

ONE

Hinduism among the World's Religions

Hinduism is like a great cultural river which flows into the ocean of world history. Derived from myriad rivulets and streams of incidental yet meaningful origin, it has gradually formed over the centuries a mighty flow into which its past particulars are still often discernible. To several hundreds of millions of Indians it is a grand inheritance, stabilizing and stimulating. Yet it also is for many the most meaningful set of values for now and for the future. It is a living religon. It is a way of life. It offers an understanding of god, the person, and society—a truly great religion. Although Hinduism historically has been largely confined to the Indian continent, it nevertheless offers its resources to any who would seek them.

Alike and Unlike

Hinduism like any other religion possesses a number of characteristic features. These are like the human fingerprint. Each person's fingerprint is uniquely his own, and from this uniqueness the individuality of the person may be determined. On the other hand, each person's fingerprint is after all a fingerprint, something that each person has. Indeed, even the fingerprints of persons can be placed into a number of basic categories for classificatory purposes. So it is with religions, although the analogue must not be pressed too hard. Religions are uniquely themselves, although they also bear some kinds of relations to each other. A religion possesses certain common characteristics which make it itself. One or more of these features may seem to be highly related to the features of another religion. But regularly it is the manner in which a religion holds a feature in relation to other components of its own essential nature that makes the particular element achieve its meaning.

Yet religions when viewed from their broader aspects do fit into some common categories. For example, in terms of the broader perspective, religions possess in common some intellectual expressions which properly may be termed *theology*. Such developments aim at analyzing reality from the standpoint of cogency and meaningfulness. Man, from a religious stance, seeks to understand his existence. Second, religions possess in common some practical expressions which properly may be termed *worship*. Intellectual formulations of religion result in doctrines, creeds, myths, propositions. In worship, however, there is action. The religious person who is worshiping seeks to express his sense of the holy which reality contains. He utilizes rituals, prayers, attitudes, sacraments, and other acts which accomplish his purpose. Religions, then, are characterized by belief and by action. Third, however, religions possess in common some associational aspects which properly may be termed *community*. Admittedly religion has its highly personal or individual aspects and moments. But fundamentally religion implies social relationships. Religion accepts some group as the embodiment of its values, the center of its understanding and action. This group may be a most inclusive social body, such as a nation, or it may constitute a special group within a larger body, as is true, for example, of Christianity and Buddhism. Religion, then, in its common features is comprised of belief, action, and belonging.

Hinduism is a religion which, as described, possesses these three fundamental characteristics along with other religions. It does have a life which is centered upon intellectual formulations. Worship is clearly a part of its very nature. And Hinduism also features a defined sense of the community of belonging. These elements Hinduism shares with other religions, although in each and every case the exact content of this sharing must be examined in detail in order that accuracy and particularity are necessarily respected.

Aside from the ways in which a religion shares common features with other religions, there are also ways in which it may be said in broad terms to possess relatively characteristic elements, especially when it is compared to other religions. In the fingerprint analogue, various degrees of commonality and uniqueness exist. For a religion the fullest understanding is largely achieved when both of these degrees or possibilities are considered. Thus it is well in this introductory chapter to spend some time in reviewing a few special or characteristic features of Hinduism as a religion. Not all of these special features need be portrayed, but pointing to two may well increase the appreciation of Hinduism as a major faith of the world.

Size

Hinduism's adherents are so numerous that it places as one of the most populous of the world's religions. It is not possible with any degree of surety to give a specific number. Nor is it possible to provide accurate statistics for any of the other religions. In fact, it is not even possible to give accurate statistics regarding the population of India itself, although there is some agreement among those who study such matters that India's population is now about 490 million. What makes Hinduism such a populous religion, obviously, is the fact that it is the religion of the largest number of people in India—some say 85 percent of the people are Hindu. If these simple figures are anywhere near true, then Hinduism is one of the world's larger religions. Probably it ranks near the very top along with Christianity, Confucianism, Islam, and Buddhism.

It is interesting to note, when viewing Hinduism as a major religion in size, that not all religions are able to attract great numbers of people. Zoroastrianism, for example, whose truth-seeking wise men are familiar to every one acquainted with the Christmas story, originated in Persia some 2,500 years ago, but today its adherents number about 100,000, chiefly the Parsees of India. Again, Jainism, an equally old religion, founded in India, and which has laid such great stress upon the importance of the sanctity of all life, today numbers only about a million members, who almost wholly are in India. Sikhism, founded in India about the time of the Protestant Reformation in Europe with the primary aim of unifying existing religions, never gained more than about four million members. These religions stand on the other end of the scale from Hinduism. They indicate that Hinduism is one of the world's truly successful religions in terms of securing and holding members.

Any elucidation of the size of religions, however, must in all honesty take a number of limits into account. The validity of religions is not to be weighed. Whether a religion is true or false, if these are categories that one wishes to bring to religions, is not dependent upon the size of its membership. The appeal of religions rests on factors other than quantity. Also, many formally registered members of a religion may hold only a nominal relationship to the religion. Membership does not in itself provide a guide to fervency. Often, as is well known and is the case in Hinduism as well, membership is reckoned on the basis of citizenship rather than a deliberate act of choice. Membership in a religion, moreover, from the standpoint of some religions, such as Judaism, Christianity, and Islam, for example, is considered as an exclusive status. That is, one can or should belong to only one religion at a time. The idea that one can be a member of two or more religions at the same time is not consonant with Western ideas. But this situation does not hold elsewhere. Thus in Japan, for instance, one may be related to more than one tradition at one time. One may pay reverence to Shinto, the immemorial national religion, and to Buddhism, a religion that historically originated in India. Hinduism, as will be seen, has been highly hospitable to other religions and its adherents are permitted wide latitude in their beliefs and practices. For these and other reasons, emphasis merely upon membership in a religion does not tell the whole story.

Yet it is accurate to say that Hinduism is a large and appealing religion. During the course of its life it has gained the acceptance of many hundreds of millions of persons. By any standard this is no small achievement; its success needs to be recognized as such.

Not every one in India, however, is Hindu in outlook. While about 85 percent are Hindus, roughly 10 percent are Muslims, 2 percent Christians, 1.7 percent Sikhs, .06 Buddhists, .05 Jains, .03 Zoroastrians, and small numbers are Jews.

Judaism, Christianity, and Islam have had long and complicated relations with India and with its religions. Some scholars assert, for example, that present-day Jews in India are descendants of the captives who were deported to Babylon after the fall of Jerusalem about 600 B.C. to Nebuchadnezzar. It may be that the town of Gozan in Media, mentioned in II Kings 18:11, is the same town known as Balhi in Sanskrit literature. Probably Jewish traders visited India in various periods of time, as such items of note in Jewish annals indicate: peacocks, ivory, apes, rice, sandalwood, and aloes. It well may be that Solomon used precious stones from India in the building of his famous temple.

Christianity, according to certain sources, developed a relationship with India almost from its organized inception, perhaps even before it established its relationship with Rome. According to the second- or third-century apocryphal Syriac document *The Acts of Judas Thomas,* the Apostles who were gathered in Jerusalem after the ascension of the Christ cast lots to determine where each would go to preach the gospel. It fell to Thomas to go to India.

Legend has it that Thomas was sold as a slave to an Indian merchant, was taken to India, and there proceeded to convert many, including the local king and many plain people. Having traveled extensively in his missionary activities, including, some say, to China, he was martyred in A.D. 72 at Mylapore, near Madras, where today a shrine honors his memory, although his remains, it is claimed, were later exhumed and transported to Ortona in Italy. The vitality of Thomas's heritage is attested to in early church writings, although the long course of Christian development in India is largely obscured until modern times.

The modern phase of Christianity in India is probably no more than five or six hundred years old. In this period, as today, a curious paradox has taken place. Christianity has never appealed to large numbers of Indians. So today there are only some twelve million Christians in that land of about five hundred million. These Christians, moreover, are roughly divided evenly between Protestants and Roman Catholics, although the number who trace their Christianity directly to Thomas are significant. While small in numbers, Christians have been a strong cultural influence in the life of India. It is not surprising that Hinduism itself, which has always been notably open to other faiths, has been influenced in its concepts and practices by Christianity. But the way in which a number of modern Hindu reformers have openly advocated Christian values indicates the influence of the Christian faith. Obviously, too, with the imperial period in India, the conjoining of English and other national cultures in which Christianity had a major share with the traditional society of India created an influence for Christianity which is noteworthy.

Islam probably has had more influence upon India and, therefore, upon Hinduism than any other faith. So deep and far-reaching has been the influence of Islam that when Great Britain withdrew according to promise in 1947, imperial India could not maintain itself but became divided, accompanied by vast violence, into two nations: India, which is predominantly Hindu, and Pakistan, both east and west, which is chiefly Muslim. East Pakistan, of course, is now the new nation of Bangladesh. Yet even in India today there are many millions of Muslims and the impact, historically, of Islam is almost everywhere in evidence.

This great influence of Islam upon India did not develop over night. It began shortly after the death of Muhammad (or in A.D. 632) when armed forces of the Arabian faith entered India, advanced as far as Baluchistan, seizing the frontier towns of what is usually called Hindustan. Going on from there, they moved to the east and finally to the south. The various political rivalries of the Hindu leaders encouraged the Muslim takeover. By the tenth century A.D., Mahmud of Ghazni (A.D. 998-1030) invaded India seventeen times and extended Muslim control to large regions, especially including the Punjab. During the sultanate of Muhammad ibn Tughlak (A.D. 1325-1351) Muslim influence extended even further. Under Akbar (A.D. 1556-1605) the Islamic empire reached its greatest geographic coverage. Akbar was an unusually talented ruler who managed to bring notable harmony among a wide diversity of Indian states and rulers and who took a position of marked tolerance toward other faiths. In fact, he tried during his lifetime to bring the various religions together into a single one, called Din-i-Ilahi, or Divine Faith, although the effort did not succeed.

There is hardly an area of life in India where the Muslim influence has not penetrated. Although they introduced Persian as a language and in a sense created Hindustani in many parts of the north, which was widely received, the Muslims also gave support to the vernaculars, such as Telugu and Tamil, encouraging the growth of literatures in these and other languages. Their knowledge in the sciences also added to India's resources. In astronomy alone they introduced the calculation of the latitudes and longitudes, created a number of observatories throughout India, and contributed various items to the calendar. They were concerned with the medical theories of the Arabs and utilized chemistry, such as the metallic acids, in their technologies. It is true that the Muslim leaders often destroyed Hindu shrines and temples. It is said, for example, that Aurangzeb (A.D. 1658-1707) in the year 1679 alone razed sixty-six temples in Amber, sixty-three in Chitor, and 103 at Udaipur. But the Muslims also gave India their own architecture and buildings. Some of the Islamic mosques represent even today some of the architectural masterpieces of India's heritage. In these and other ways, Islam has been a major influence in the long life of India. In religion Islam greatly influenced Hinduism, so that it may be asserted that no effort to reform and revitalize Hinduism following the Muslim invasions of India could neglect or ignore that great religion.

Age

Hinduism is one of the oldest, if not the oldest, of the world's living religions. Some religions by reason of their founding dates cannot claim great antiquity. Sikhism, for example, may be dated from A.D. 1469, the birthdate of Nanak, its founder. It is perhaps the last or latest of the various religions that have been founded throughout the ages. Disputes over what constitutes a religion may create differences as to the acceptance of later formulations. Islam, a religion by almost everyone's count, is also relatively recent in its inception, the date usually given being that of Muhammad's birthdate, A.D. 570. Christianity similarly cannot be compared with Hinduism in age. Whether the birthdate of Jesus was A.D. 1 or 4 B.C. or some other date, according to the varying views of scholars, there is relative certainty regarding the start of that religion.

While approximate historical starting points may be given for religions, such as those just suggested, it is also clear that religions often bear a close and even intertwined relationship with religions that predate them. Hence the question of the precise origin of a religion is more obscure that actual dates may suggest. Thus Sikhism was founded by Nanak in A.D. 1469, but in point of fact Nanak sought to combine an already existing religious heritage, principally Hinduism and Islam. He did form a new religion, but the features of his new religion are those taken from religions of even greater antiquity. So it is with Islam and Christianity. Islam bears a close relationship historically to both Christianity and Judaism, both of which predated it. Christianity, no matter what its founding date, cannot be understood without reference to Judaism, which preceded it through the course of many centuries.

If one leaves the Christian era and looks further for religions of even greater age, the phenomena of the seventh and sixth centuries B.C. present fascinating and impressive evidence. No period in human history shows a comparable creativity in the founding of religions. In that era a number of religions were born which are still significant forces in regional and world culture. Confucianism came into existence about 551 B.C., the approximate birthdate of Confucius. Buddhism was created about 560 B.C., when Gautama the Buddha was born. About 599 B.C., Vardhamana, or Mahavira as he is better known, founded Jainism. Taoism, a religion found almost exclusively in China, was originated by Lao-Tze and is usually given the founding date of 604 B.C. And Shinto, which some of its adherents say had no point of inception in time, is commonly dated to the time of the first Japanese emperor, 660 B.C., Zoroastrianism was also possibly founded in 660 B.C. Despite the debates that are held regarding the accuracy of these dates, it is possible to state that the seventh and sixth centuries B.C. were indeed highly productive of religious forms and of religions themselves.

Judaism, although founded earlier than these religious expressions, also at a roughly comparable time was enjoying a new burst of creativity. This was the time of the great Babylonian prophets: Jeremiah, Ezekiel, and the Isaiah of the exile. In Greece, moreover, in the sixth century B.C. there was a religious development which some scholars have called revolutionary. It consisted of the divinely inspired seers—including the shamans, sibyls, Pythias, Bacchants, and orphics—of the state cults, including the mysteries at Eleusis and those of the heroes whose most tangible symbol was a temple or shrine, and the most controversial of all, the monsters, variously known as sphinxes and sirens, of contemporary art. Prior to this period, moreover, philosophy also was very active; during the lifetime of Mahavira, for example, early Greek philosophers also were teaching: Thales, Anaximander, Anaximenes, Xenophanes, Pythagoras, and Heraclitus.

Judaism and Hinduism are two of the oldest religions still alive. Both are practically impossible to date with any acceptable degree of accuracy. Judaism may have originated with Moses from 1500 to 1200 B.C. Hinduism may have originated from 2500 to 1500 B.C. Both religions had antecedents and, as already suggested, it is difficult indeed to know when a genuinely new social form comes into existence. No matter how one settles the views of scholars who disagree on almost all matters of the dating of the origins of religions, it seems reasonably clear that Hinduism is a very old religion, one of the oldest, and perhaps the oldest.

In asserting the antiquity of Hinduism, moreover, it is well to note that Hinduism is a living religion. All the religions that have been formally discussed thus far are living religions with the exception of the Greek religion of the sixth century B.C. Obviously there are other kinds of religions. One other type of religion is that which is dead, which does not remain a presently organized form of religious life. Probably more religions have been born and have died than have stayed alive. Nothing apparently guarantees a religion its life. Religions come and go—even those which anciently have appealed to large numbers of adherents and which at the time might have been supposed to be imperishable. Among the dead religions one thinks immediately of the religion of the Greeks and the Romans. But there are others: the religions of ancient Mexico and Peru, of ancient Egypt, Mithraism, Manicheism, of the early Teutons and Scandinavians, of Babylonia and Phoenicia, of a host of peoples mentioned in the Bible. Many religions have come into existence, have served well and lasted long, but in our time are largely matters of historical curiosity and scholarship.

Another category of religion is that of the primitives. Many religions of primitive peoples still exist and have their proper role in the study of universal religion. Yet these religions, like their peoples, have not been widely influential. They have appealed to relatively small groups of people. Commonly, moreover, they do not have sacred scriptures, mainly because almost by definition primitive peoples are those without writing. Primitive religions regularly do not have more than a tribal base for their appeal, and although other religions, the more advanced, may also appeal to special communities, as was mentioned earlier, they usually involve elements which transcend a purely tribal foundation. Hinduism by most definitions is not a dead religion, but is one which is thoroughly alive and pertinent to its adherents and others. Hinduism also is not a primitive religion or the religion of a primitive people. It is a highly complex religion which is an expression of a highly complex culture, an advanced culture of the present time.

Religions commonly are not overly interested in dates and chronologies. Because of their nature they often assume a kind of timelessness about themselves. Religions view themselves as possessing more than transient insights into things. They are almost by definition aimed at penetrating the nature of ultimate reality. What they perceive to be the truths that pertain to this reality are hardly deemed to be mere vocal or literary evanescences. Religions assume that they are dealing with the permanent, the underlying, the fundamental. So religions regularly assume that the truths which they represent have been from all time and that little value is gained by trying to search for origins.

This respect for ancientness and timelessness is apparent in Hinduism as well as in the other religions. This characteristic in Hinduism is called *sanatva*, or ancientness. Hindus have great respect for the antiquity of their religion. The old is good. That which is old and, therefore, good is oftentimes above reproach. It is revered because it is old, and because of its age it tends to secure widespread acceptance. The social codes, rituals, beliefs, and associations of Hindus are considered to comprise a sacred way of life; they are the *sanatana dharma*, or eternal law of the faith.

No doubt exists, as will be shown later, that many contributions were made to Hinduism, some from tribes and groups that originally inhabited the land of India. But the rich contributions from foreign sources also must be acknowledged, especially by scholars, although both kinds of contributions tend to be minimized in number and extent by the orthodox faithful. The claim of antiquity, then, becomes a simplifying one, denying the sort of complexity and ambiguity which is the expectancy and even the delight of serious students of the origins of a religion.

Hinduism, then, qualifies as a major religion among the world's religions. Although born in very ancient times and like a great river fed from innumerable sources, it became an identifiable, complex faith for many millions of peoples. These peoples are almost entirely confined to that land area which prior to British withdrawal in 1947 was imperial India. Today these peoples are found mainly in the present-day, democratic India and to a lesser extent in the present-day Pakistan and Bangladesh. The influence of Hinduism, however, is less geographically confined and may be found in other parts of Southeast Asia and indeed in various parts of the Western world as well. As a living religion, Hinduism also has survived many challenges to its existence, has experienced times of dormancy and renewal, and has maintained itself through a remarkable flexibility until today. Currently it is undergoing change, but this change is essentially a wide-scaled adaptation to modern and oftentimes secular conditions. Hardly anyone with knowledge of the history of the religion believes that it will not survive. Its vitality, a consequence of its ability to meet human needs, will undoubtedly enable it to continue indefinitely as a major religious force in India and in the world.

An attempt to describe and define the full nature of Hinduism has not been undertaken in this chapter. That highly complex task is in reality the subject of the whole book. Various approaches to the fullest understanding of the nature of Hinduism will be made in the various chapters. Thus, by exploring Hinduism's history, certain aspects of its nature will be explicated. History is the subject of Chapter 2. Chapter 3 more directly seeks to analyze the major components of the religion, although themes touched upon there will be developed at greater length where they are more appropriate to the unfolding story. Again, Chapter 4 discusses the nature of Hindu philosophy. The intellectual aspects of Hinduism comprise another facet of the total religion which bears on the theme of definition. Popular religion, discussed in Chapter 6, relates yet another feature of the nature of the religion. Thus in these chapters and elsewhere throughout this book the nature of Hinduism is described from a variety of perspectives.

TWO

History

The history of Hinduism is broadly the history of India. No simple scheme exists by which several thousands of years of historic events can be organized and traced with certainty and clarity. Yet Hinduism in its history did evolve through a number of historical stages or eras that may be discerned both by nonreligious happenings and by those which gave a distinctive character to the religion. Thus in seeking the origins of Hinduism it is clear that a major point of differentiation occurred with the migration of the Aryans into India and the development of Vedic religion. The period prior to the Aryans and the Vedas constitutes one unit of Hindu history; the Vedic period constitutes yet another. Each will be described briefly prior to the effort to delineate the history of the post-Vedic period.

Although the history of Hinduism and that of India are inextricably intertwined, only certain general aspects of the history of Hinduism are included in this chapter. The political history of India, to pick merely one illustration, is not developed here, although it comprises a fascinating story in itself. Other aspects of the total history of India similarly cannot be undertaken here, for reasons of economy of presentation. Obviously, too, the history of Hinduism presented in this chapter is simply a sketch which is aimed at providing the general reader with some sense of the totality of this limited aspect of India's whole history.

Pre-Vedic Period

The pre-Vedic history of Hinduism may be broadly divided into two other periods: the pre-Dravidian and the Dravidian. In the pre-Dravidian period the earliest known human life in India occurred. One of the earliest known tribes is the Negrito, who were surely among the earliest inhabitants. They, however, were not indigenous to India, but made their way into the land from Africa. It has been suggested that they were a dwarfish group who traveled into India through Arabia, that is, by land. Even today among some of the primitive tribes of south India, traces of the Negrito may be found. These tribes include those of Madras and Travancore, eastern Assam, and even some of the aborigines of the Andaman Islands. It is known that they were concerned with life after death, thinking, for example, that the path to paradise is guarded by a fierce demon. Their animism included fish, plants and animals, and especially the pipal tree (a kind of fig tree). Although they were primarily food-gatherers, they also used the bow and arrow.

The Austric peoples also are among India's earliest settlers. Somewhat larger than the Negrito, probably of eastern Mediterranean origin and known sometimes as Proto-Australoids, they too left a lasting influence upon later India and Hinduism. The Austrics represented a more developed culture; they were acquainted with fairly advanced agricultural methods, the use of the outrigger canoe, the blowgun, the domestication of fowl and horses, and other signs of advancement. In religion the Austrics were also more advanced. They developed creation myths and especially the idea of the world being born from an egg. They had a cosmology in which time was told by phases of the moon and recognition was made of the Pleiades. Possibly the idea of *karma*, the cosmic distribution of justice whereby a person's status in life is determined by previous existences, originated with them. The introduction of the cult of the phallus, prominent in later Hinduism, is Austric even to the point of the adoption of the Proto-Australoid word *linga*, which means arrow, stick, and phallus. In these and other ways the Austrics were important culture-makers in the pre-Dravidian period.

The Dravidian period in Indian and Hindu history is of considerable importance, for the Dravidians brought to India a more settled and advanced culture which in relationship to the civilization brought by the Aryans largely constituted the broad framework in which India developed and in which Hinduism as a highly formed religion came into being. The Dravidians, like the Negrito and the Austrics, were immigrant peoples. Some scholars hold that they came from Mediterranean sources and that they constituted one of two branches. One finally migrated to Mesopotamia and became known in history as the Sumerians; the other went to India by way of south Persia and the Makran coast. While the name Dravidian pertains to a migratory people, it also connotes a group of languages spoken by some of the peoples in early and southern India: Tamil, Kanarese, Telugu, Malayalam, and others. Although the Dravidians, of course, spoke a non-Aryan language, they had a significant influence upon the later Indo-Iranian languages and especially on Vedic and Sanskrit.

Knowing the nature of the Dravidian culture was greatly aided by archeological excavations that began in 1922, and have continued since, of certain parts of the Indus valley and the Punjab. The excavations uncovered the cities of Harappa, Mohenjo-daro, and Chanhu-daro. Harappa was located on the Ravi River and was the prehistoric capital of the Punjab. Mohenjo-daro was situated on the Indus River about 400 miles to the southwest in Sind. Chanhu-daro was located in the same area. Clearly the Dravidians possessed a highly developed urban civilization. Some parts of the

Vedas, the earliest scriptures of Hinduism, tend to derogate the Dravidians. But the Dravidians were far from being barbarians; they possessed many of the features of a highly developed people. One of the handicaps in knowing more about the Dravidians from the Mohenjo-daro–Harappa excavations is the fact that so far no one has been able to decipher their writing. But they were literate. Practically all that is known has been derived from the physical arrangements and artifacts of the cities and the iconographical remains.

The Dravidians brought a fairly well-developed culture with them to India. In architecture, for example, they apparently impressed the pre-Dravidians with their ability to build two- and three-story houses and buildings. They utilized stone, bricks, and iron in their construction, built fortresses and mansions, and generally provided a base upon which the Aryans later developed their own buildings. In the creation of villages also the Dravidians were skilled and contributed to the Aryans. They knew how to organize communities; build trunk roads; make drains, water-wheels, and wells; and generally to conduct a successful agriculture.

The Dravidians, moreover, made lasting contributions in religion. It well may be that the majority of the people of India today are of Dravidian stock and a large number, if not a majority again, of the total retain features of Dravidian religion. This is especially true of the south Indians. Certainly the name and the form of the most widespread household worship, the *puja*, are of Dravidian origin. Great numbers of Indians address non-Aryan and Dravidian deities. The zoomorphic deities of current Hinduism, such as Ganesa, Garuda, and Hanuman, are of Dravidian origin, as are such important deities of Aryan inheritance as Siva and Vishnu. Even Krishna, one of the most appealing of the Hindu deities, is probably of pre-Aryan beginnings. Thus in social and economic organization, and especially in religion, the Dravidians provided a most significant set of contributions to the ongoing life of India and of Hinduism.

Vedic Period

The Vedic period in the history of Hinduism, following upon the pre-Vedic, constitutes one of the most formative and influential eras. It had many consequences, but one of the most noteworthy was the creation of Vedism, that religion of the Aryans which became normative for all later Hinduism. The Vedic period saw the formulation of the fundamental character of Hinduism, the basic configurations of which are powerfully apparent even to this day in India.

The term *Aryan*, which figures so large in the Vedic period, is properly assigned to a family of Indo-European peoples only one part of which should be thought of in relation to India. The cognate term, for example, survives today for another part of the family in the modern name for the nation Iran. No one for a surety knows from whence the Aryans came; possibly they came from central Asia or some parts of the Soviet Union. One group in its migration turned west and became the forerunners of the Greeks. Thus the whole history of the Aryans is highly complex, and the group which found its way into India comprises only one part of the total.

The very word *arya*, the base for Aryan, means *noble*, and the Aryans, to themselves, were noble. They were light-skinned, tall, generally blue-eyed people who used copper, iron, and bronze to maintain their pastoral society. They spoke an Aryan language, which in India ultimately became Vedic which in turn developed into other languages. The Aryans themselves had a system of nobility in which elected chiefs governed village or tribal groups through a council.

Time's distance does not permit strict accuracy in recounting the history of the Aryan invasions of India. But there is evidence that points to the possibility that about 1500 B.C. a number of related Aryan tribes came into India through the northwestern mountain passes, mainly through the valleys of the Gomal, Kurram, Kabal, and Swat rivers. Their invasion was not always met with resistance, but at times it was the requirement for their conquest and domination of the indigenous peoples. In the early period they swept through the Indus and Gangetic plains. Later they moved on toward Assam and Bengal. Much later they were able to move deeper into southern India, the province of the Dravidians, but only after some centuries had passed. The story of the conquest of southern India is told in part in a famous Hindu classic, the Ramayana. In time, however, the Aryans, with their culture modified by those which they met, became the dominant peoples in India.

Important for the present purpose is the religion of the period of the invasion: Vedism. Vedism appropriately is known in large part through the sacred scriptures of the Aryans which are termed the Vedas. The Vedas probably do not date to the very time of the Aryan conquest, that is, about 1500 B.C. Rather, the Vedas were formed in interaction with the religion and culture of the pre-Vedic period. Perhaps the Vedas should be dated to about 1000 B.C. At any rate, they are among the oldest known religious texts in the world. They provide, moreover, the best single source for an understanding of Hinduism in this most important period of its formation.

The sacred scriptures of Hinduism are divided into two categories: the *sruti* and the *smriti*. The *sruti*, meaning "that which was heard," corresponds to the idea of revealed teachings that is found in other religions. Along with the Vedas, the Brahmanas and the Upanishads comprise the *sruti* of Hinduism. This class of scripture is revered as *apaurusheya*, or "not of human origin." They are thought by Hindus to be even more imperishable than the deities, for while the deities may come and go the *sruti* is eternal, infallible, and absolutely basic to a valid concept of reality, including human life. In one version the *sruti* reveals the knowledge (Vedas, from the root *vid*, "know") which has been revealed by the primal deity, Brahma, the self-existent and all-knowing.

The *smriti* category of scriptures, meaning "that which is remembered," corresponds to the auxiliary literature of other religions. In Hinduism the *smriti* scriptures are highly complex in themselves and are definitely secondary to the *sruti*. The *smriti* scriptures are usually classified into five types: Vedangas, or "limbs" of the Vedas; Dharma Sastras, or the codes of laws, commentaries, digests, and manuals; Nibandhas, or writings devoted to rituals and domestic rites; Puranas, or scriptures of popular Hinduism; and the epics which relate the heroic tales of Hindu mythology and history. In addition, there are other kinds of *smriti* literature.

The Vedas, the subject of attention at this time, are found in four collections of hymns, verses, and formulas for performing sacrifices: the Rig Veda, the Yajur Veda, the Sama Veda, and the Atharva Veda. Clearly the Rig Veda is the most important. It offers 1,028 hymns in a form that aids recitation. Their organization reflects the deities that are extolled and the families of seers who have celebrated them. The Yajur Veda features descriptions of ancient sacrifices, many from pre-Vedic times. The Sama Veda is similar to the Rig Veda and is arranged for musical rendering. The Atharva Veda, which some Hindus have felt to be so inferior to the other three as not to merit the designation of *sruti*, consists of hymns for the daily life of believers.

The Vedas are revered by Hindus as being of divine origin and authority. For them names are used which ordinarily are employed to describe the gods. But their earthly and practical nature is a consequence of the activities of the *rishis*, or seers. In Vedic times the *rishis* were unusually sensitive and respected religious leaders who received the revelations that had Brahma as their source. The *rishis* in a sense comprise the personal founders of the religion of Vedism and of later Hinduism. They played a highly significant part in the development of Hinduism.

The Vedas consist of collections of hymns, various verses, and sacrificial prescriptions. The term *samhita* connotes *collection* and is variously used to describe the character of the compilation and at times is synonymous for the whole body of the Vedas. *Samhita* also refers to the poetical portions of the Vedas, which are thought to be their core.

The term *Vedas* also is employed in a more inclusive sense. Aside from the four basic collections, the concept also includes for some the Brahmanas, a later set of scriptures, and the Aranyakas, or forest documents, which are attached to the Brahmanas and used by hermits in their reclusive meditations. Within the Vedas, moreover, those parts which are metrical psalms are called the *mantras*. These are believed to be the most ancient parts of the Vedas and are, therefore, the chief corpus of the *samhita*. Obviously the idea of *samhita* means that the Vedas lack a consistently logical organization or development; they are collections of materials of varying age and value.

Like some other sacred scriptures of other religions, the Vedas were not written down in their original or present form and given intact to the ages. They were handed down historically in oral form by many holy men and teachers who took occasion to amplify, correct, and otherwise change their early form. Not until about 200 B.C. was the present text fixed. Probably the Yajur, the Sama, and the Atharva Vedas were more improvised historically than the Rig Veda. In fact, memorization of the Vedas and other scriptures was held to be a high virtue, and many times in Indian history the writing down of the scriptures was taken to be an evil. A later scripture, the Mahabharata, for example, condemned to hell anyone who sought to write it down. Part of the explanation of the defense of the oral tradition was based on the theory that learning the Vedas and other scriptures by hearing them and committing them thusly to memory was a more meaningful way of learning. For many centuries, learning by hearing rather than reading was held to be the essence of the learning process itself. Without the availability of written documents the rise of any critical investigation of the scriptures of Hinduism was retarded until relatively recent times. Then such analysis was largely begun by Western scholars who brought to the documents a different interpretation of the meaning of learning. Despite historical and scholarly qualifications, however, the Vedas are looked upon by Hindus as being truly sacred; they are the *sruti* scriptures. Reverence for the Vedas, on the other hand, does not mean that most Hindus are closely attached in practical ways to the Vedas. Written in an ancient variant (Vedic) of a so-called dead language (Sanskrit), the Vedas are more held in respect than they are in fact used by most Hindus.

Nature worship is a key element in early Vedism. The Vedic worshipers were concerned with natural phenomena, such as how does a brown cow give white milk, how does the sun stay in the sky without support, and how can the water of the rivers continually pour into the sea without the sea overflowing. While several of the hymns of the Rig Veda appear to be monotheistic in accent, the people of the Vedic period were polytheistic. They worshiped many gods: Agni, the god of fire; Parjanya, a rain deity; Surya, the sun god; Ushas, goddess of the dawn; Yama, god of death; and many others. An unsophisticated animism also existed in which divine powers were attributed to specific natural objects and events.

Temples, idols, and priests seem not to have been a part of early Vedic religion. The *yagasala*, or place of worship, was not designated and worship could take place almost anywhere. Temples were introduced in the later Vedic period. Since the gods and goddesses were everywhere, there was little necessity in the early period to make idols. The priests appear to have been the religious servants of the chiefs and in the early period were not dominant in the social system.

The Vedic period was not one of personal and social restraint through religion. The Vedic Aryans loved life thoroughly. While later the killing of the cow and the eating of meat were taboo, the Vedic period saw no such limits; the Aryans killed animals and ate meat freely. They loved music, dancing, hunting and fishing, gambling, and drinking of intoxicating beverages. The family was mainly monogamous and women had a share of responsibility in the performance of the sacrifices as well as in other matters. Child marriage and the prohibition against remarriage were not known in this time. In the early hymns of the Rig Veda, moreover, the phallic worship of the pre-Vedic period was condemned.

Great respect was shown to *rita*, which is the order of natural events, a primitive kind of scientific causation, and at times the moral ordering of life. What a man sowed, the doctrine went, so he also would reap. This view of the moral life was mirrored in the natural world. Although the Rig Veda does not mention the transmigration of souls, a doctrine to become prominent in later Hinduism, it did assert that the virtuous man would find a place in a heaven and that the unvirtuous man would be assigned beyond death to a dark place.

Appended to the Vedic period was an era of which the Brahmanas, another *sruti* scripture, were an embodiment. The Brahmanas reflect a time when the priests developed significance beyond what they held in the Vedic era. The Brahmanas indicate that priestly religion had made serious inroads into the relatively less formalized religion of the Vedic peoples. The Atharva Veda, by its emphasis on magical formulations, was a precursor. The Brahmanas, dating perhaps to 600 B.C., are theological and priestly manuals which assumed great powers for the brahmins, or the priestly class. They serve in part also as commentaries on the Vedas and in part as very detailed descriptions of the exact ways in which ceremonies were to be performed. They lay stress upon the importance of the caste system, which is a prime indication that this system was by this time already a significant reality. The Brahmanas signalize the end of a long period of time, the closing of a fundamental period in the growth of Hinduism, the apogee of a religion that began in loose and simple ways to a point in which rigidification and formality reigned.

Another class of literature appears at the end of the Brahmanas. It consists of the "Forest Treatises," or the Aranyakas. These treatises also are related to the Vedas and extol the mysteries of nature, the responsibilities of earth-bound man, and the form of his destiny in the next life. They are meditative in character and are intended for use by anchorites who have withdrawn from active life and who spend their time in the forests thinking on ultimate things. Only four of the Aranyakas are extant, but they form a link between the preceding Brahmanas and the succeeding Upanishads.

It is formally appropriate to distinguish between the Vedas, the Brahmanas, the Aranyakas, and the Upanishads, for they are widely recognized as being separate developments of Hinduism's literature. But they also should be viewed as a continuum, that is, they are highly interrelated and interdependent. They must be considered the early and growing branches of a single treetrunk which is Hinduism itself.

Reaction

For some centuries following the Vedic period, Hinduism changed and grew under what might be termed a spirit of reaction. Vedic religion was in a sense maximal religion. It believed a great deal. It saw religious forces almost everywhere, and in time these forces came under the control of a fourfold caste system in which the brahmins, or priests, became clearly dominant. The Brahmanas epitomized this development. The need to modify the overdevelopment of ritualistic, polytheistic, brahmin-controlled Vedism became so evident that a variety of efforts took place over a period of centuries, perhaps from 600 B.C. to 200 B.C. Hinduism can be understood in that time largely in terms of the "protestant principle," a reaction against the dominant orthodoxy. This reaction took many forms, which in themselves constitute a long and involved story. Only several elements of this history may be profitably reviewed here with the hope that as illustrations they will show some of the major lines of development. The following, then, will be briefly described: the Upanishads, Buddhism and Jainism, and the *nastika* contributions.

The Upanishads represent a major philosophic response to Vedic religion. Although the Upanishads are considered by Hindus as a part of the *sruti* scriptures, they represent in a basic sense a contrast to the prior writings. They seek to portray a religion which is not mired in ritualism and priestly domination. They represent, moreover, the first genuine effort in Hinduism to rest the religion in a philosophy or theology. This philosophy is not systematic, as philosophy is often found in the West. Rather, it is intuitive. Yet it is appealing in its subtlety and refinement. Because the philosophy of the Upanishads is essentially thoughtful and even recondite, it is not greatly appealing to the mass of Hindus.

The Upanishads, meaning "near-sitting," developed as lectures that were given to special students of the time who sat near their gurus, or teachers, to give attention to the sacred word. Probably this teaching was done between 400 B.C. and 200 B.C. The primary emphasis in the Vedas is upon activities of a religious character; in the Upanishads the stress is upon knowledge. The Vedanta, a later form of Hinduism, is based as a system of knowledge upon the Upanishads.

Although the Upanishads do not present a single doctrine, and some of them reflect some of the elements in the Vedic tradition, they do seek to grapple with some of the most pressing philosophic issues of their time or any time. They are concerned with the nature of ultimate reality, with the relationship of man to it and of men to other men, the basis and purpose of human existence, and a plan of salvation.

The Upanishads teach the existence of Brahma, the all-encompassing, self-existent, eternal, immutable, and single reality who is without attributes. Only Brahma is truly real. All else, all phenomena of the sensate world, are *maya*, or illusionary. *Maya* comes about because of ignorance or lack of knowledge. *Karma*, or moral causality, thus is necessary in human affairs to control imperfection. The cycle of birth-death-rebirth of the world of phenomenal existence, or *samsara*, can be broken only by a true knowledge of Brahma and the truths dependent upon him. Salvation, then, is possible, although far from easy. The individual soul, or *atman*, is mutable and subject to constant change. But the *atman* also possesses an identity with Brahma. By this means the Upanishads significantly tie the essence of the person with the essence of reality, namely Brahma.

The individual Upanishads vary in length and quality. Perhaps 150 major Upanishads exist, although usually a number near one hundred is taken as the extent of the best. Of these an even smaller number, which varies according to the interpreter, is said to be principal texts.

The value of the Upanishads is essentially twofold. First, they represent an effort to define a religion in contrast to the religion of the Vedic period. Second, and most important, they constitute a first-rate formulation by means of an intuitive philosophy of the intellectual aspects of Hinduism. As such the Upanishads have been greatly influential in the whole course of Hinduism's growth, and today are viewed with appreciation and even reverence.

Both Buddhism and Jainism may be viewed basically as reactions against a highly sacerdotal Hinduism. Although both Gautama, the founder of Buddhism (*ca.* 568-483 B.C.), and Vardhamana, the founder of Jainism (*ca.* 599-467 B.C.), succeeded in giving such impetus to their views that later gave birth to independent religions, they began within the context of Hinduism. The religions which they founded cannot be fully understood without an appreciation of their own reaction against ritualistic Hinduism. Gautama's faith was directed toward finding release from a world of misery. In his effort he did not teach the existence of a god, did not engage in worship practices, and is not known to have prayed. He taught the Four Noble Truths: that all existence involves suffering; that suffering is caused by giving in to insatiable desires; that suffering will cease when such desires are controlled; and that while still alive the person should live moderately. He called men to join a *sangha,* or sacred community of believers; in this *sangha* there was no place for Hinduism's rigid caste system. Gautama maintained the doctrine of *karma,* the illusion of selfhood, the transmigration of souls, and also the doctrine of *nirvana,* a state of utter happiness in which the person is freed from all limitations. This religion, seized upon over the centuries by many millions, in part was formed in reaction to the Hinduism of Gautama's lifetime.

Jainism also sought to modify the existing Hinduism and cannot be fully understood except as in part a reaction against Hinduism. Although Vardhamana, like Gautama, was born to status and luxury, he taught that the way of salvation from the miseries of this life lay in asceticism. Like Guatama, Vardhamana did not teach the existence of a deity. He also condemned the caste system and brought his followers into a *sangha*, or casteless congregation. He believed in the moral law of retribution (*karma*) and called upon his followers to be ascetic, quiet, accepting, unobtrusive, and kindly. Jainism greatly stressed the doctrine of *ahimsa* (noninjury to any living thing). Thus Jainism represents another and important effort to reform Hinduism even though it issued in yet another religion.

The remarkable elasticity of Hinduism is illustrated by its ability to withstand the development of Buddhism, Jainism, and other movements which were aimed at reforming the religion. The reactive movements were successful to a surprising degree, for Hinduism has always been a most open and receptive religion. Yet in the case of Buddhism and Jainism (later also of Sikhism), independent religions also were formed as offshoots. In fact, Hinduism has mothered three religions, a number that even surpasses Judaism, which gave birth to both Christianity and Islam.

In this same historic period a number of unorthodox sects grew up in India and are termed *nastikas* or "deniers." These groups were known at least by the time of Gautama and Vardhamana and they continued for some centuries. They were mainly known for what they denied in contrast to the *astikas*, who were the "asserters" or those who put their beliefs in positive form. One of the founders of *nastika* thought was Brihaspati, who denied the existence of the gods, the existence of revelation, the obligation of moral codes, the necessity for political authority, and many other standards of traditional Hinduism. Other *nastikas* inveighed against Vedic religion with its elaborate sacrifices, its plethora of deities, great and small, its dominance by the brahmins, and its allegedly absurd view of the world. They held that pleasure alone was the final norm for conduct, since all other moral teachings reflected the devices by which the strong ruled the weak. They denied the great philosophic formulations of the Upanishads on the grounds that the only knowledge available to men is that which derives from their senses. Thus philosophically they espoused a kind a sensationalism and materialism. The *nastikas*, then, are significant in their own right, but they also constitute a reaction against the overbeliefs of the traditional Hinduism of the Vedic period.

Medieval Period

Following the period of creative reaction to the religion of the Vedic period came an era, long and varied, in which Hinduism in part recovered its strength of appeal and in which many new developments occurred.

Hinduism's remarkable capacity to absorb influences upon it with ease and indeed even with profit was not missed on the various movements of reaction. The Upanishads with their strong philosophic appeal filled a genuine lack in the totality of Hinduism. They became one of the *sruti* scriptures and to this day are a primal part of the religion. The reformists, Gautama and Vardhamana, seeking to purify the excesses of Vedic ritualism, had their effect upon Hinduism, but in turn they also became the founders of new but related faiths. The *nastika* thinkers tended to reduce the easy belief of many Hindus, yet they also in time went their own ways. Hinduism, then, recovered from these thrusts and in fact was strengthened by them. For centuries, perhaps as many as fifteen in all, Hinduism did not suffer from a lessened attractiveness, but was able to maintain itself with the masses.

The medieval period, however, was not without its more expressive developments. From time to time new forms of the faith appeared and stimulated loyal Hindus to fresh understandings of their traditions. The rise of several important sectarian movements breathed a new air into the routinely accepted religion. Two of these may be mentioned as illustrations: Vaishnavism and Saivism.

The origins of Vaishnavism are uncertain, but it is known to be a vital force in Hinduism in the medieval period. The sect constituted a religious form of Hinduism in which Vishnu, a major deity in the Hindu pantheon, was the chief object of worship along with his two chief incarnations, Rama and Krishna, and their consorts. Members of the sect have claimed that their form of Hinduism goes back to the Vedas and to the Upanishads. Almost any strand of Hinduism can be traced to the Vedas, however, so in this case there does not seem to be unusually persuasive reason to make this assumption. Also, the idea of the worship of Vishnu and others is scarcely enjoined in the Upanishads where the traditional forms of worship are surely not advocated at all. Probably the formulation of Vaishnavism was derived more from the practices of the Hindus of their own time—from the influences upon Hinduism generally from the groups and tribes which were historically present at the start of the medieval era.

Vaishnavism has a number of distinctive traits. It primarily lays great stress upon the importance of *bhakti,* or devotion to a personal god of grace. It represents a highly personalized faith in which the believer gains salvation through his individual relations with a deity who is readily available to him through incarnation and by simple ritual. The believer, thus, is urged to surrender himself completely through a mystical experience to the being of Vishnu and others, and through this surrender to find peace of mind. Vaishnavism, following this concept of religion, embodied other elements, such as an antibrahminicalism. The personal factor in the faith allowed no greater validity for the authoritative mediation of the priests. Again the sect also emphasized the importance of the vernacular languages: Hindi, Tamil, and Marathi. Sanskrit as the ancient and venerable language was by this time not spoken by the masses. The use of the vernaculars provided the faithful with an opportunity to communicate freely. The Vaishnavites at first were strongly opposed to the traditional ritual. That ritual was viewed as a barrier to the highly personalized relationships with the deities that formed the basis for the sect in the first place. But in time a degree of ritualism was readmitted, although it was distinctively Vaishnavite, including the use of caste marks. As might be expected, Vaishnavism as a Hindu sect gave birth to various subsects, such as the Haridasa, the Sahajiya, and the Kisori-bhaja, each with its own special definitions and practices.

Saivism is another development within the medieval period. A sect, like Vaishnavism, its origins are not entirely clear. It also is centered in the worship of a deity, Siva and his symbols. Saivites are usually more demanding of themselves than are Vaishnavites. They are strongly ascetic and believe in the mortification of the flesh. It is the Saivite, for example, that most commonly gives the picture of the Indian lying on a bed of nails. In fact, the Saivites also practice various kinds of perversions and depravities, such as haunting cemeteries, feeding on excrement and carrion, covering their bodies with cow dung, and venerating the *linga*. The Saivites, on the other hand, are monotheistic, holding themselves above the polytheism which surrounds them. They worship no idols, although they do wear religious necklaces. Saivites also are marked by a deep sense of personal sin. The idea that all believers are unworthy because of moral inadequacies is probably connected with some of the baser personal practices which seek to mortify the body and the person. Like Vaishnavism, Saivism through the centuries of its development gave birth to a number of subsects, such as the Pasupata, the Saiva-Siddantas, and the Kashmir-Saivites. Although Vaishnavism and Saivism were not major innovations in the history of Hinduism, they are important in themselves and as examples of the steady growth of the religion in the medieval age.

Sikhism represents a significant development of the late medieval period at a time when Islam was already on the Indian scene as a major challenger to traditional Hinduism. Although Islam had entered the life of India only some twenty years after the death of Muhammad, or in the seventh century A.D., its fullest growth did not occur for centuries. At the time of Nanak (A.D. 1469-1538), the founder of Sikhism, Islam was a major and widespread religious and cultural force in India.

Nanak was born in a small village about thirty miles from the capital of the Punjab, Lahore. Although his family was Hindu, his father worked for a Muslim. Heeding what he considered to be a divine call, Nanak began a lifetime of journeys, especially in northern India, to preach his new word. Believing that a higher truth was available through revelation than that which was embodied in both Hinduism and Islam, Nanak taught the essentials of what in time became not a unifying religion of the existing two, but a third religion, called Sikhism (from the Sanskrit word *shiksha,* for disciple or learner). Like Gautama and Vardhamana, many centuries before, Nanak was an influence upon Hinduism, but finally his cause was transformed into an independent religion.

Nanak's teachings owe much to an earlier reformer, Kabir (A.D. 1440-1518), who criticized both Islam and Hinduism, denounced idolatry, and sought to set aside the Vedic traditions in general. Nanak, however, gave his own distinctive impress to the new faith. He taught that there is only one deity. Emphasis was strongly placed upon the repetition of the true name of the deity. The value of the repetition of the name of god was thought to be equal to the value of a religious pilgrimage, a significant virtue in Hinduism. Salvation is to be found in god and through the repetition of his name, which is True. The world is viewed in Sikhism as being of little value and the person is conceived to be so helpless and inadequate that only through identification with the one god is salvation to be found. The helpless person needs religiously to be taught by a guru, or teacher. The importance of the guru is great in Sikhism, although this stress is mirrored both in Hinduism and in Islam. Like Buddhism and Jainism, Sikhism organized the faithful, the *khalsa,* or pure, in a casteless congregation, called the *sangat.* Within the congregation idols and sacrifices were prohibited. The Vedas were not accepted as authoritative by the Sikhs, although their own sacred scriptures, the Adi Granth, not only took the place of the Vedas but became in time so highly venerated that the charge of idolatry has been made regarding its acceptance and use. Thus, through the efforts of Nanak, who was followed by ten revered gurus of stature, Sikhism, which began in part as an effort to reform Hinduism or certain features of Hinduism, became in itself an independent religion, the third in a sense to have been mothered by Hinduism.

The reader must bear in mind that only a mere sketch of Hinduism's history is being presented here. Mainly the accent is upon some of the main features of the religious development of India. Much more remains to be said, although by design it will not be said here. Any writing on the history of Hinduism or of India, for they are coterminous, necessarily suffers at the present time from a lack of adequate historiography. This lack may be explained in several ways. Hinduism, for example, is not a historical religion in the sense that the Semitic religions are historically aware. The Semitic religions, mainly Judaism, Christianity, and Islam, lay considerable stress on history's meaningfulness. History is an arena of the divine presence and purpose. Other cultures, moreover, such as Egyptian, Greek, and Chinese, also were historically minded for other reasons. But Indians traditionally have lacked a well-developed historical sense and concern. They have tended to look upon the concrete events of history as being of only momentary importance and hardly worthy of detailed record.

Again, while India today is clearly a nation-state, it historically has been a highly diversified collection of various peoples and cultures. The idea of a national history does not come easily to India. Caste also tended to restrict the broader historical interests of Indians, for they were primarily interested in their own castes and histories rather than in the history of a total people. The highly developed poetical and fantasy-oriented character of the Indian peoples historically also made mythopoetics more attractive than the keeping of hard facts concerning chronological developments.

The sacred scriptures of Hinduism contain few verifiable facts of history. Undoubtedly there are many concrete facts of a historical nature that are embedded within the scriptures, but these must be interpreted or inferred; they are not adequate for an understanding, say, of the chronological succession of rulers or other specific matters. One exception is contained in the Puranas, the Yoga Purana of about 50 B.C., although even this record can scarcely be classified as history as understood in the West, since it is so heavily burdened with clearly mythical and religious elements. Several noncanonical histories also exist, but these too would not meet modern standards of historiography. In addition, much of what is dependably known was accomplished in the recent decades by Western scholars. Indian historiography today is a most inviting field of study on the part of professionally trained historians.

Modern Period

The modern period in Hinduism's history, like the prior eras, is difficult to delineate chronologically. Each designation of historical periods, of course, is artificial and is meant only to provide rough approximations of changes within Hinduism. Sikhism stands, for example, within both the medieval and the modern periods. The modern period, however, possesses a number of characteristics in addition to that of recency. In the modern period a revived sense of the meaning of Hinduism came into being. In part this development was a consequence of the growth of Indology, that is, the scholarly study of India's history, literature, languages, and religion. Indology, strangely enough, was initiated by Western scholars principally. Its beginnings date to the seventeenth-century Dutch missionary, Abraham Roger, who wrote commentaries on Hinduism, especially upon the brahmins of his day, and the eighteenth-century Jesuit, Johann Hanxleden, who wrote the first Sanskrit grammar (in Latin), although it was not published. From that time on and with increasing effectiveness non-Indian scholars developed the study of India itself. Later, of course, the subject became a principal concern of Indians and particularly those who were interested in Hinduism. In the modern period of Hinduism's history the study of antiquities related to the faith became prominent and is in fact one of the main features of the modern period.

The rise of nationalism in India also contributed to an awareness of the importance of Hinduism, which, after all, has always been essentially a national religion. Nationalism as it was stimulated by India's experience with the various national imperialisms became a strong impetus to the revival of Hinduism as an intrinsic part of the national definition. The modern and universalizing culture, moreover, consisting of education, faster modes of travel, awareness of the larger world, the impact of the technologies, and the rise of other national states, all gave revived interest and indeed compellingness to the study of Hinduism, as well as other matters.

The modern period also has been characterized by a large number of efforts to reform and revitalize Hinduism. These efforts have been a consequence in part of the fact that Hinduism, like other religions in the modern world, has had to engage in vigorous activity in order to maintain its relevancy and cogency. The process of secularization, which has been so apparent in the West, has also been part and parcel of the experience of the East.

Many reformers have made important contributions to the revitalization of Hinduism in the modern era. The largest number, of course, cannot be portrayed here, since the present purpose is not that of providing a comprehensive or an exhaustive review of Hinduism's history. Three reformers of note, however, will be mentioned briefly as illustrative of the larger number: Ram Mohun Roy, Dayananda, and Ramakrishna.

Ram Mohun Roy (A.D. 1772-1833) has been termed the father of modern India. Through his intellectual and spiritual qualities and his ability to organize effectively he became a leading reformer of modern Hinduism. Born in Bengal, the son of an orthodox brahmin family, he was early impressed religiously (in 1811) when he witnessed the rite of suttee, or *sati,* in which his brother's wife was burned to death, over her strong objections, on the funeral pyre of his brother. The impact of this experience was so powerful that he later campaigned against the practice and considered his success, when the British banned it, as a major lifetime accomplishment. In his early life he had the advantage of good education; he knew and used some eight languages. He studied the Koran, the sacred scriptures of Islam, and developed a hatred for idolatry. He became a revenue official in Rangpur, where he both worked and held discussion groups on religion in the evenings until he decided at the age of forty-two to resign and devote himself completely to religious activities.

In 1828 Roy founded the Brahmo Samaj, or Society of God. At its inception the organization was intended to embrace any and all who believed in the one god of all religions, but in the main it attracted only Hindus who appreciated the stress on a personal theism. Congregational worship, including the use of hymns, was a feature of the Brahmo Samaj, and in the place of worship no idols were permitted, and no sacrifices took place. The new society appealed to many, including the famous, such as Debendranath Tagore (A.D. 1817-1905) who, following Roy's death, led the society to stress Hinduism less and Indian nationalism more, and Keshab Chandra Sen (A.D. 1834-1884), who modified it even further by making it more Christian than Hindu.

The Christian emphasis of the Brahmo Samaj was not foreign to Roy. In 1820, for example, he published a booklet on the precepts of Jesus as the guide to peace and happiness. Roy was greatly impressed by the Christian missionaries and particularly by the four Gospels. But Roy's interests also were strongly social. He sought to reform Hinduism as a support for a variety of social practices in India which he deplored. He supported the improvement of the status of women by opposing child marriages, polygamy, *sati,* and the generally low status of women. He believed that public education was essential for the modernization of India and fought for it. He opposed the caste system and looked toward the day when all persons regardless of their situation at birth would have equal opportunity for advancement and happiness. All these social goals Roy supported with impressive zeal, and he and his followers secured considerable influence with the masses and with the Indian governments.

Roy is buried in Bristol, England, where he died while on an official mission. In England he was received by the House of Commons, Jeremy Bentham, and other organizations and persons with great respect.

Dayananda (A.D. 1824-1883) was born into a wealthy Saivite family of brahmin status. Inducted into the brahmin caste at eight years of age, he began to develop doubts about various aspects of traditional Hinduism. He was deeply worried, for example, because as a youth he saw rats eating the sacrificial offerings in a Saivite temple and wondered how Siva as well as the believers could permit such desecration. Later Dayananda suffered the death of his sister, to whom he was closely attached, and an uncle. This led him to speculation regarding the meaning of life and death. His inherited religion was not helpful. Troubled by such experiences, and even while the preparations for his marriage were underway, he left home and wandered about India. He discussed religion with the *sannyasins,* or ascetics, deepened his knowledge of the Vedas, and concluded that much of the Hinduism of his day was corrupt. A blind swami, or teacher, Virajananda of Mathura, had a profound effect upon his life, teaching him again from the Vedas and calling upon him to revive Hinduism by teaching the purified Vedic texts and preaching the Vedic faith with new vigor. In 1875 in Bombay he founded one of the most influential movements of the modern period, the Arya Samaj, the Noble Society.

Dayananda regarded the Vedas as the only true key to the meaning of life. In order to call people "back to the Vedas" he gave up preaching in Sanskrit, taking the Hindi language of the masses as his own. He condemned idolatry, even in the sacred city of Banaras. But he also taught that Sanskrit was the parent language of international culture and that through it all peoples had received a deposit of truth. The Vedas, moreover, were regarded as the fountainhead of all knowledge, sacred and secular. His disciples regularly sought to find even modern inventions, like the steam engine, television, and the existence of microbes, mirrored in the hidden passages of the Vedas. Although he accepted the doctrines of *karma* and transmigration of souls, he developed a highly sophisticated philosophy of monism, asserting, for example, that the soul is free from the absolute or Brahma, contrary to the teachings of the Upanishads. The Arya Samaj grew and prospered, influencing the nature of modern Hinduism for many Indians.

Ramakrishna (A.D. 1836-1886), born a brahmin in Bengal, was a highly sensitive spirit. From an early age he was intensely interested in religion, serving, for example, as a temple priest, or *pujari,* in a temple devoted to the black goddess Kali at Dakshinesvar, which is near Calcutta. His elder brother was the chief priest of this temple. All his life he suffered from states of exhilaration and depression; twice in later life he attempted suicide. Also, he was prone to have trances, to be in states of coma; perhaps he was an epileptic. Although his family arranged that he marry a girl of five when he was twenty-five, he never lived with the bride; she returned to her father's house and he stayed at the temple. Throughout his life, Ramakrishna was repulsed by sexuality and wished for no contact with women. Yet he idealized all women, making them into mother figures in part and also viewing them as embodiments of his favorite deity, Kali.

Ramakrishna was for a long period of his life almost totally immersed in worship of Kali. He believed that he was in direct communion with her and spent his hours in prayer, singing, and mystical devotion. She was so real and available to him that he neglected his temple duties and lost his position. In retirement in a neighboring wood he continued his worship of Kali. He then met a *bhairavi,* or mendicant nun, who instructed him further in devotion to Kali, providing him with certain *sadhanas,* or magical techniques, and yogic exercises. Somewhat later he took instruction from an itinerant monk, Totapuri, who initiated him as a *sannyasin* (holy person) and gave him the title of Ramakrishna. Prior to that he was known by his family name of Gadadhar Chatto- padhyaya. Later his disciples added the title Paramahamsa, which means "supremely holy." By that time he had also undergone other visions of the deities, including one with Krishna.

In fact Ramakrishna sought directly to experience relationships with a variety of religious personages, some of whom were from other religions. He studied Islam and said that he was able to accept that religion. He sought to achieve a mystical relationship with Muhammad and claimed that he succeeded. Similarly he was greatly attracted to Christianity, studied it, and claimed that he received a personal vision of the Christ. Ramakrishna never for- mally espoused any other religion for himself than Hinduism. But he did believe that all religions are true: Hinduism, Islam, Chris- tianity, and others. One of his ways of stating this view was to say that fish tastes differently with various modes of cooking or preparation. So religion everywhere is the same; only the external features are different and god honors all expressions of worship. He was in effect a pantheist, seeing god in all things.

Ramakrishna died of cancer at the age of fifty. His wife, Sarada- devi, who lived to 1920, was considered a saint and was worshiped by his followers. The cause of Ramakrishna might not have suc- ceeded so well, however, had not his chief disciple, Vivekenanda (A.D. 1863-1902), taken up his mantle. While Ramakrishna was not strong in learning, scarcely spoke his own Bengali well, and had disdain for intellectual formulations of religion, Vivekenanda, on the other hand, was a highly intellectual and articulate person. He traveled through India and indeed to the United States by way of many other countries and spoke to a meeting in Chicago of the World Parliament of Religions in a highly persuasive manner. Vivekenanda taught that Christ, Buddha, Krishna, Ramakrishna, and others were all incarnations of the one, supreme god, like bubbles produced on the cosmic sea.

Ramakrishna, Dayananda, and Ram Mohun Roy are simply three of the many persons who both reformed and revitalized Hinduism in its modern period. The process still goes on. Hinduism today contains many vital sectors of active faith which with intelligence, social vision, and devotion seek to keep the religion at the core of the individual and collective life of Indians. Hinduism has shown its ability to survive over the ages. From time to time it has been challenged with seemingly new and startling innovations and even schisms. But Hinduism is a remarkably adaptive religion, shifting its feet to secure firmer foundations as the winds of change seek to shake it. It has survived many influences of a widely varying nature and there is little reason to think that it will not be capable of meeting the challenges of the present time.

At the present time Hinduism continues to undergo a variety of challenges and developments. These are expressive of the impact of modern culture on India and thus on Hinduism. Yet they also contain the bases for the continued revitalization of the faith. Only three out of a much larger number will be mentioned here as illustrations. First, Hinduism is developing a notable degree of self-consciousness. As India has become an important national state on the international scene, Hinduism for many Indians remains as the primal component of national identity. India and Hinduism have been intertwined for many centuries, but the nationhood of India today looks to Hinduism as providing a proper and proud form of cultural outlook. The separation of imperial India from England and the formation of two nations, India and Pakistan (now three), tended to accentuate the distinctiveness of both Hinduism and Islam. Hindus became more aware of themselves, often with a degree of hostility which violated some strands of the historical faith that stressed tolerance and openness. It is true that such elements as democracy and socialism comprise important ingredients in India's national ideology, but nevertheless Hinduism for many provides currently the most significant single form of identity. And well it may, for the other elements in India's culture have been introduced only in relatively recent times. Hinduism is the ancient, binding cultural expression that has weathered the centuries.

Second, Hinduism has produced a notable number of leading figures in India's present life. The modern reformers previously mentioned fall into this category. But there are others. One of the most preeminent of recent times was Mohandas Gandhi (1869-1948). This great politician and reformer contributed markedly to the development of Indian national self-consciousness. He provided more than anyone else the initiatives which led to the independence of present-day India. Yet Gandhi was a political reformer who based his political appeal and vision largely on the basis of religious and ethical precepts. This fusion of religion and politics led to important practical consequences, but it also led to the increased respect of many Indians for their traditions. Here was a leading figure who found revolutionary ideas within the tradition of Hinduism and applied them to achieve notable results. In addition to Gandhi, other Indian leaders in recent times have been congenially oriented toward Hinduism. Sarvepalli Radhakrishnan, a former president of India, possessed an international reputation as a leading scholar of Hinduism, and his writings are still widely respected both within India and without. Beyond politics, moreover, there has existed in recent times in India a large number of leaders in other walks of life who have sought to express their creativity within the context of Hinduism.

Third, Hinduism is responding with some success to the inroads of westernization and secularization. These social processes have made serious modifications of traditional life for many Indians. The growth of industrialization, for example, has greatly modified the traditional exclusiveness of the caste system. It no longer is possible for an Indian to separate himself from others in modern means of transportation. Again, the requirements of the assembly-line type of production is no respecter of caste rigidities. The Indian who dines out cannot maintain his caste restrictions on the preparation and serving of food. In these and other ways, traditional requirements in Hinduism are bending to the necessities of an increasingly westernized and secularized society. On the other hand, present-day Hindus often seek in modifying their religious heritage to reaffirm the essential importance of the faith. For example, while education is more widespread in India than ever in the past, it tends for many to provide the basis upon which the intellect may be applied to the search for solutions suitable to the Indian experience of modernization plus an adherence to tradition. Hindus with their heightened self-consciousness also see in their religion some of the bases for resisting or modifying the full impact of westernization and secularization. They are less prone to think that these universal processes will automatically or dogmatically bring the fulfillment of life for all Indians. This dialectical process of acknowledgment and resistance may well shape a truly distinctive national culture in the India of the future. On the extreme, moreover, there are such orthodox Hindu groups as the Mahasabha and the Rashtrya Swayamasevak Sangh which seek to overcome the constitutional separation of religion and the state and make Hinduism the official religion of India. Their cause, however, does not have prospects of success. Whatever the future, Hinduism as always will probably possess the resources for remaining a key element in India's life.

THREE

$\mathcal{N}ature$

Hinduism is perhaps the most diverse, complex, open-ended, ambiguous religion known to man. Part of its complexity rests upon the rich and varied history of India. The existence of many contributing tribes and peoples in the broad geographic expanse of India also constitutes a factor. The relationships which the Indians have had with a variety of foreign peoples through travel is another part of the explanation. The fact, moreover, that Hinduism has no personal founder is an additional consideration. Other reasons for this complexity also exist.

Founder

Hinduism is a religion without a personal founder. This is both a disvalue and a value. In this regard, Hinduism is somewhat distinctive. Several of the other living religions are characterized by personal founders; in fact, the largest number are associated with a personality who is revered as founder. Three religions have taken the name of their founders into their titles: Confucianism, Muhammadanism, and Zoroastrianism, named, of course, for Confucius, Muhammad, and Zoroaster. In a sense, however, Muhammadanism is simply one of the major terms of reference for the religion which Muhammad founded. The other and perhaps more prevalent term is Islam. So Muhammadanism may be considered a doubtful case. Islam, meaning "submission," designates a principal characteristic of that religion, the idea that the believer should be submissive to the one, true god. Islam, as a name for a religion, is indicative of the fact that another group of religions has taken a theme or a main teaching of the religion as its official designation. Thus Shinto means "the way of the gods," Taoism, "the way," and Sikhism, the religion of "the disciples." Although Shinto is not known to have a personal founder, both Taoism (Lao-Tze) and Sikhism (Nanak) do.

Other religions have secured their names from an attribute of their founders' lives or teachings, or both. Buddhism, while founded by Gautama, is so named because Gautama taught the significance of "enlightenment" and he himself attained to that blessed state in his own life. Similarly, while Jainism was founded by Vardhamana, it takes its name from *jina*, the "conqueror." The Jain is one who is a spiritual conqueror. Vardhamana, as the founder of Jainism, moreover, is called Mahavira, or "a great-lived-one." Christianity is an interesting appellation in that it in part refers to the Christ as well as being a more systematic terminology. The founder of Christianity, of course, was Jesus. The state which he achieved was that of being "the anointed one," or the "messiah." So it is an attribute of the founder which in this case has been taken up into the title of the religion. Judaism as a name is quite distinctive. No other one word exists to designate the totality of this religion, its history, life, and teachings. The first usage apparently occurred in Greek-Jewish literature about 100 B.C. Thus it may be found in II Maccabees 2:21; 8:1; 14:38. This designation also is found in the New Testament in Galatians 1:13.

Hinduism refers to the religion of the Hindus. Both *Hindu* and *India* are of foreign derivation. The term *India* is derived from the ancient Indo-European word *Sindhu,* which was given by the Aryans to indicate the western boundary of their early conquest, the Indu River; *Sindhu* means *river.* Later the Persians pronounced the word as *Hindhu* and used it to designate the people themselves rather than the river. The Greeks later dropped the hard-sounding aspirate, changing it to *Indos,* while later both they and the Romans employed the term *India* to refer to the northern section of the continent. Hind and Hindustan are a contribution of the post-Islamic and Persian periods.

Although Hinduism does not possess a single founding father of the religion, it does recognize the importance of inspired leaders, especially in early, or Vedic, times. These leaders are termed *rishis,* or seers. The *rishi* is a person who is able to exercise wide influence among his fellows because of his unusual wisdom and religious powers. Often the *rishi* expressed himself through literature. Thus many of the hymns of the Vedas were composed by them. It is commonly assumed that Valmiki created the Ramayana and that Vyasa developed the Mahabharata. Sometimes the *rishis* went about doing good, such as when they ended droughts or healed sick persons. But sometimes they were described as irascible and threatening beings. They are pictured in the Hindu literature as being vengeful toward persons they disliked. On the other hand, they are recognized, too, as often being related to the deities and as taking part in various supernatural events. In Vedic times particularly the *rishis* constituted a rich source of creativity and inspiration for the development of Hinduism.

Geography

Although Hinduism offers no personal founder, it suffers, if at all, not from a narrowly defined nature, but from its very complexity. This complexity bears explanation. The geography of

India is a factor. Present-day India is the seventh largest country in the world, possessing a land frontier of over 9,400 miles and a coastline of over 3,500 miles. This large expanse is divided into three main areas. First, in the north, close by the great mountains, lies a large area of high altitude, varied topography and distinctive human enterprise. Further south is the Indo-Gangetic plains, formed by three river systems, rich and fertile, the home of the largest number of Indians. Between Delhi and Calcutta, for example, nearly one thousand miles apart, there is a drop in elevation of only about 750 feet. Third, there is the southern peninsula, which is a fairly high plateau with coastal strips. These three divisions of the land have meant historically that at least three major Indian developments have been made possible. The peoples who have lived within these regions, adapting themselves to the land, have achieved relatively distinctive cultures.

Languages

The geographically encouraged complexity of India is further exemplified by its languages. Today in addition to English, which is widely spoken and used in university, governmental, commercial, and other relations, there are fourteen major languages and about 250 dialects. This fact means that India even today does not enjoy a single language through which all the people of the nation may communicate with each other. In north India the common languages are Punjabi, Gujarati, Oriya, and Bengali. Most of north India's inhabitants also understand, and some speak, Hindi. This language is the single most widespread language in India; perhaps half of the population speak or understand it, often as a language in addition to their own. The Dravidian-derived languages of south India—Telugu, Kannada, Tamil, and Malayalam—bear small resemblance to Hindi.

The Vedic language is ancient and classical, not presently used, but is significant because it is the language in which the revered

Vedas were written. It perhaps was derived from what scholars call Proto-Aryan, a common ancestor of a number of old languages. The Vedic language also was a precursor of Sanskrit, another highly important classical language. Sanskrit was relatively late in developing in India, probably being formed about 300 B.C. The religious works whose value makes Sanskrit also valuable even today were written at a later time, perhaps centuries later. Sanskrit was never a widely spoken language; mainly it was the medium of the scholar. Those who wished to communicate religious truths often failed to employ Sanskrit. Gautama, for example, taught in the vernacular. The official edicts of many of the Indian rulers were promulgated in languages of the people. Kabir (A.D. 1440-1518), one of Hinduism's powerful reformers, said that Sanskrit is like the water of a well, while the vernaculars are like the waters of a flowing stream. He spoke wisely, for while Sanskrit is highly revered by many and has indeed made a significant contribution to the literature of India, it is not, and perhaps never was, a vitally living language for the many. Tracings of Sanskrit, however, are to be found in many of the current languages in use in India.

Travel

The complexity of Indian life and of Hinduism, its central system of values, is reflected by the contributions made through the travels of Indians. At first glance the very geography of India seems to be a formidable barrier to travel beyond the borders. The mountains and the oceans by which India is surrounded have restricted the movement of Indians to other places and indeed of other peoples into India. Yet these barriers, while great, have not been entirely controlling. Actually the ancient Indians were great travelers. They traveled for a variety of reasons, aside from the sheer pleasure which travel brings to many. They enjoyed commercial relations far beyond their native land. The ancient peoples of the Indus valley were familiar with the civilizations of Egypt, the Middle East, and Asia. The merchants made their way to Assyria and Babylonia, bringing teak for the temples of these peoples and other supplies as well. Indians also traveled as mercenaries in the service of other nations. Greek sources, for example, mention that Indians fought with Alexander the Great in his effort to subdue the peoples of the Indus valley, that they were present in the army of Darius the Great, and even formed a whole division within the forces of Xerxes. Similarly Roman writers tell about the commercial and military activities of the Indians. Virgil, for example, records that Indian soldiers fought under Antony and Cleopatra at Actium. So, records from various parts of Asia tell of Indians who traveled, sometimes settling, in China and southeast Asia. The Indians, therefore, despite the geographic barriers to travel, were in fact rather renowned travelers, taking the goods and ideas of India to far-away places and returning with goods and ideas that influenced the life of India.

In all fairness, however, it must be said that a strong sentiment against travel also has existed in India. Until recently orthodox Hindus were discouraged from travel. The prohibition extended not only to travel abroad, but also to travel within the country. This restraint tended to work against the religious purposes of Hinduism in which pilgrimages to holy places are considered a religious obligation. But the ban on travel was mainly enforced, paradoxically, by the brahmins themselves. Apparently with the revival of brahmanism in the early centuries of the Christian era the restriction on travel was viewed as yet another means of enforcing the authority of that caste and of limiting the outlook of the pious. This restriction, however, also limited the brahmins, so that the brahmins of Chedi, for example, could not travel to the land of Vidarbha. If they did, as was true of nonbrahmins, they would be considered unclean and would have to undergo the *prayaschitta,* or ceremony of purification. The carryover of this prohibition occurs today when some orthodox Hindus will not travel by ship from India on the *kalapani,* or "black waters," for fear that they will become unclean.

Flexibility

As a religion Hinduism is remarkably flexible, permissive, and inclusive in its outlook and nature. This truth is one of the chief characteristics of the religion. This attribute accounts in no small measure for its unparalleled complexity. Many persons who have grown up in a culture in which the religions of Judaism, Christianity, and Islam have been a central and traditional force find it difficult to believe that a religion could exist that is so genial toward variety and differences. They reflect the fact that these three religions, used as examples, have taken the viewpoint, enforced in various ways, that they and they alone are the final and autonomous norms of religiosity. One is assumed to be a believer ideally only when one swears sole and final obedience to the one faith. This finality of faith is somewhat tempered in the case of Christianity insofar as its fundaments rest on Judaism, although the relations between the two religions as found in their followers are not always harmonious or simple to conceive. Even in being closely related there are factors that drive the faithful apart. The long history of anti-Semitism and anti-Judaism within Christian groups is striking and clear evidence of the strain. While Jews and Christians bear a historical relation in matters of faith, they are not always able to come to terms with each other in actuality. So it is with Muslims and Christians and between Muslims and Jews. Each of the three religions is closely intertwined with the others, yet each finds it difficult to develop constructive and accepting relations with the other. This phenomenon derives, it is here claimed, from the faith that each of these religions shares, a highly discernible trait, namely, that each religion affirms that it is the sole and final form of faith. Each can basically tolerate no challenge to that assertion. No other religion can even share in the making of that conviction. Of course, within each religion, and especially in more recent times, there are those who are able to be more flexible, permissive, and inclusive.

Hinduism historically stands in great contrast to the imperial claims of Judaism, Christianity, and Islam. It has always maintained a most conspicuous attitude of tolerance and appreciation for other religions. Few leaders within Hinduism's history have taught that it is the one and final faith for all mankind. Quite the opposite is true. Hinduism has not only expressed repeatedly its attitude toward other religions as one of complete acceptance, it has demonstrated this willingness by openly affirming the validity of other religions. Hinduism, with the exception of a few groups within it, has traditionally been a nonmissionary religion. It has not sought to convert non-Hindus to Hinduism. Hinduism has taken over the centuries a "live and let live" attitude toward the question of who possesses the sole and final truth.

What in general terms might be the sources of this attitude? This is a proper, although a difficult, question to answer. The very diversity of religious expression within Hinduism itself may have led its adherents to develop a spirit of understanding and acceptance regarding outside faiths. A broadly interpreted doctrine of *karma*, a kind of predestination, may also be a factor. Thus the Hindu takes the position toward life that there is a principle regulating individual, physical, and moral matters in which a binding and purposeful causality is controlling. It may be that even religions come under this *karma,* that whatever shall be the final truth will be established by cosmic regulation rather than by human initiative. Again, the Hindu idea of *maya* (illusion) may be a contributing factor. Many Hindus believe that all perceived reality and all human knowledge is *maya,* illusionary. This view does not necessarily disparage such reality and knowledge; it merely indicates its limits. Man is not capable of reaching the one, true reality which in actuality is Brahma, the self-existing one. Man must be content to know only limited reality. The use of the concept of *maya* as a means of understanding Hinduism's tolerance may be speculative, yet it suggests a basis on which Hindu flexibility, permissiveness, and inclusiveness may be founded. At any rate, Hinduism is not a kind of religion that believes it possesses the sole and final truth in religious matters. It does not believe that it must win out over any and all other religions. It is not a religion which seeks to bring all mankind under the sway of it *regnum*. It is not a religion which has been marked historically by relations of tension and strife with other religions. Contrariwise, Hinduism always has been ready and willing to assume its own limitations. It has been able to show respect for the faith of others. It has sought an understanding of other religions. In this regard, Hinduism is a distinctive religion.

The attitude of flexibility, permissiveness, and inclusiveness which Hinduism has held regarding other religions it also has maintained, with few exceptions, within its own community of faith. Sectarian Hindus commonly are not set in dead opposition to each other. They do not assume that one interpretation of Hinduism is better or more true than another with the consequence that the allegedly inferior view must be opposed or the person holding it must be curbed. It is assumed that every man has a right to believe as he wishes. To illustrate this situation in Hinduism, Radhakrishnan, a leading modern interpreter of Hinduism, especially to the West, has used the analogy of the various colleges which comprise Oxford University. He suggests that the several dozen colleges there are all devoted to the same end: the truth. Each at times believes earnestly that it holds more of the truth than some or all of the others. Rivalries may grow up between the colleges; some partisans may make rash statements regarding superiority and inferiority. But the truth remains, it is asserted, that each and all of the colleges comprise the university, that all are devoted to truth, that a proper attitude for one college to another (on the part of individuals or collectivities) is that of mutual respect, acceptance, and understanding. So, the argument by analogy runs, the various individuals and sects within Hinduism are each striving to apprehend the truth; each has need of the other.

A major fact regarding Hinduism, then, and one well worthy of continuous contemplative consideration, is that it is a religion without a formal doctrine of heresy. Traditionally, in Christianity, for example, heresy has played a significant role in the determination of faith and in the maintenance of the autonomy of religious bodies. It or the lack of the need to enforce it has been a key feature in the definition of orthodoxy. Heresy has primarily a negative function, that is, it exists when an assumedly revealed doctrine as determined by scripture or tradition is denied. Heresy most often pertains to dogmas of a religious body which have been specifically defined, although it may be related to truths that such a body holds in a general form. A heretic, moreover, in the Christian tradition, is one who has assumed the validity of the religious heritage through an act of baptism. A non-Christian, then, cannot be truly heretical. Again, the heretic must make his denial voluntarily. This means that a coerced denial of a dogma, by whatever means or source, is not a basis for action against the heretic. Finally, heresy is a denial of doctrine that is characterized by obstinacy. The heretic is not one who denies a doctrine and then retracts his denial. He is one who persists in denying. Hinduism, by the terms of this definition of heresy, is a religion which historically and presently permits nonconformity. Its inclusiveness excludes any systematic effort to control the beliefs of its adherents through heresy definitions and actions. No Inquisition has ever marked Hinduism's history.

Six Forms

Scholars and others have often remarked that Hinduism seems to be not so much a single religion as it is a whole set of religions, all of which are joined together by the single factor of the name of the religion. Such an assertion bears further consideration, but it does point to the astounding complexity of Hinduism. One of the chief characteristics of Hinduism surely is its internal diversity. It is a many-splendored thing. No adequate scheme of interpreting the diversity of Hinduism exists, but at least six forms or facets of the religion may be mentioned briefly to illustrate this complexity. These forms will roughly follow the development of the sacred scriptures of Hinduism in which these forms are embodied. Obviously the total complexity of Hinduism still will elude this analysis. This whole book, moreover, will hopefully provide some description of this diversity, although much that exists will not be encompassed in this volume.

First, Hinduism consists of nature worship. Although this form of Hinduism still persists in India and is the religion of countless persons, its most obvious and important source is the Vedas. These ancient works portray a religion in which hymns are addressed to many dozens of objects or beings, mostly those associated with natural functions, such as fire, rain, dawn, air, wind. The Vedic religion consists of efforts on the part of human beings to enlist the aid of the deities to secure happy homes, long life, sons, success over enemies, and other worldly gains.

Second, Hinduism consists of priestly religion. The Brahmanas epitomize this kind of religion; they still express the religion of many Hindus. Priestly Hinduism stresses the importance of ceremonial functions. It is dominated by the brahmins, who are the managers of the rituals. Sacrifices, even including bloody ones, are a part of this form. Caste is very important in this kind of Hinduism and especially the brahmin caste is important, for this caste in reality holds the key to the deities from whom human desires are satisfied.

Third, Hinduism consists of philosophy. Practically unknown in any developed sense prior to the Upanishads, this form of Hinduism has held wide appeal, especially among intellectuals, ever since. It sees the religious task as that of gaining knowledge regarding ultimate reality. By means of thought it seeks to find underlying connections between man and god. The plurality of nature deities and the importance of priestly ceremonies are not held in high esteem in philosophic Hinduism. Sometimes yogic exercises are employed as a means of clarifying the mind, but the social expression of this form often is austere.

Fourth, Hinduism consists of legal prescriptions. Sacrifices, ceremonies, and philosophic speculation have not held the loyalties of all Hindus. Many are concerned about detailed requirements for effective social functioning. They look, for example, to the religion embodied in the Laws of Manu, composed perhaps about 250 B.C., in which wise counsel is offered to parents on how to rear children, the need for children to be obedient to parents and teachers, the rules governing repentance and confession, the proper ways to eat and be married, and other matters. Appropriate relations among the castes also is a major concern of this type of Hinduism.

Fifth, Hinduism consists of devotional attitudes and exercises. The key concept here is *bhakti* (devotion). This devotion is usually expressed toward a personal deity and that personal deity most often is Krishna, whose story is most appealingly told in the Bhagavad Gita. The Gita has won almost universal appeal as a genuine classic of Hinduism. The Gita is exceptional in Hinduism for several reasons, but chief among them is the fact that for the first time the unknowable Brahma is known through a personal incarnation, Krishna. Devotion to Krishna appeals to many Hindus as the finest expression of the religious tradition.

Sixth, Hinduism consists of popular religion. All of the previously mentioned forms of Hinduism, of course, are popular, but they appeal to selected groups within the Indian population. Popular Hinduism is essentially a conglomerate in which several strands of Hinduism are conjoined. The several sects express this kind of Hinduism frequently. The devotees stress pilgrimages, which are times of religious delight and satisfaction, elaborate festivals, the recognition of the religious nature of the seasons, reverence for idols, the importance of ceremonies within the home, and obedience to the rules of caste. Two great epic scriptures support popular religion: the Mahabharata, which describes the great

Bharata war, and the Ramayana, which describes the career of a chief deity, Rama. In addition, the Puranas, which also are collections of religious tales, are important scriptures in popular religion.

These six forms of Hinduism, then, constitute some of the main expressions within a religion which in totality is Hinduism. While they have been described here in terms of basic categories, it must be borne in mind that they do not appear neatly in Indian life. Obviously, too, at many points there is overlapping.

Common Core

In the face of such variety and complexity in a religion, the question arises as to the possibility of locating the essence, its core of belief and practice which gives it its coherence. If Hinduism is in reality not one faith, but a number of faiths loosely bound together, what then is it that binds? What common elements cross the boundaries between the various forms of the religion? Of course, it must be said quickly that a religion is not a self-conscious being which feels under obligation to provide answers to questions such as have been raised. A religion is what it is. Its followers may see questions or problems within it and seek to deal with them; that is to be expected. Similarly, those outside the religion also may ask questions and seek answers to them. Obviously too, the quest to locate the essence of a religion is primarily a rational or an intellectual enterprise and many would claim that religion involves much more than that. Hinduism would affirm in several of its forms the limits of reason. Yet, despite these counterquestions, the basic question remains and intriguingly calls for some response.

Five basic elements seem, more or less, to constitute the essence of Hinduism: belief in god, reverence for the Vedas, the practice of rituals, certain ideas that govern life, and caste. Each of these will now be briefly reviewed, although each is the subject for further analysis in other parts of this volume.

First, belief in god binds Hindus together in a common faith. Probably the prior sentence should have included the phrase: "in some form," for while Hindus generally believe in a power beyond themselves which is controlling in their lives and in the lives of others, they are far from agreement as to the nature of that being. Some Hindus worship divine forces which they believe reside in various objects, processes, and persons, such as the wind, fire, fertility, holy men, and historic personages. Others limit their believing to a select number of deities which control even larger segments of life. Others, of course, believe in Brahma, the one, fully transcendent god who stands over against all the flux of phenomenal existence. Others, amazingly enough, like the *nastikas*, are either skeptical about the existence of divine beings or out-right deny their existence. Yet even these would claim to be within the Hindu tradition. The sects, moreover, are generally founded and are bound together by devotion to a particular deity, such as Siva, Vishnu, Krishna, Ganesa, or Hanuman. At times, further-more, idols may possess a potency for the believer that relates directly to the function of a belief in divinity. Thus it is possible to say that most Hindus believe in some form of deity, although beyond that qualified statement other statements must be made in order adequately to describe the situation.

Second, reverence for the Vedas binds Hindus together in a common faith. Regarding this element, as with all of the elements that are being suggested as common-denominator factors in Hindu-ism, a positive statement of considerable validity may be made, but it must be immediately followed by a series of delimiting qualifications. The Vedas are held in the highest regard by the largest number of Hindus. They are the *sruti*, or most truly re-vealed scriptures available to them. Most Hindus, no matter what they actually believe, rest their belief on the Vedas, and the Vedas are sufficiently rich and comprehensive, as well as ambiguous and suggestive, that practically all manner of belief may be referred successfully to them. Yet the Vedas comprise only a part of the *sruti* scriptures. The Brahmanas and the Upanishads also are held to be similarly inspired. They are books of holy guidance to many Hindus. Those of a philosophical bent, for example, are more favorably oriented toward the Upanishads perhaps than to any other scripture offered by Hinduism. Again, the orthodox sectarian groups often are more devoted to their own *agamas,* or scriptures, than they are to the Vedas, although they may not deny their respect for the Vedas. Among many modern Hindus, moreover, belief in the Vedas takes the form of quite human appreciation for the documents as comprising a key part of the national and religious heritage. From this standpoint the Vedas are viewed basically as literature, much in the same sense that the Christian Bible is taught in American colleges as literature. Hindus, then, tend to be bound together by reverence for the Vedas.

Third, the practice of rituals binds Hindus together in a common faith. Rituals form a major part of the cultus of Hinduism as rituals do for other religions. The loyal Hindu, for example, marks the various stages of his personal growth by *samskaras,* or sacraments. These make meaningful for him and others the years of his past and the hopes for his future. Other rituals are related to daily life within the home. For example, part of the noonday meal is offered to all of the gods, a libation of water mixed with sesame is also made in recognition of the dead, and so forth. So from birth to death the Hindu faithfully performs a large number of rituals. Hinduism for most Hindus is a highly ritualistic religion. The ritualism, however, is not largely centered in the temple, but is chiefly a feature of family and community life. Hindus differ in the number of rituals which they practice; some practice a great number, while others find ritualism distasteful. Hindus may differ in the nature of their ritualistic practice; some rituals are recognized by some and not recognized by others, who will have their own. But ritualism is an element which binds Hindus together within their one great faith.

Fourth, certain ideas that govern life bind Hindus together in a common faith. One of the most widely accepted doctrines of Hinduism is that of *karma. Karma* asserts that every human action or intention makes its own imprint upon the personality. Human thoughts and acts are not lost, they do not simply evaporate, as though they did not matter ultimately. The case is just the opposite. All human wishes and activities leave an imperishable deposit with the ongoing person. A person is what he thinks and does. The consequences of each intention and action may come upon the individual in this life or it may come to fruition in a later life. But *karma* signifies a causally moral, cosmically based, law of retribution. It is a basic principle of Hindu life, one which binds Hindus together.

The doctrine of the transmigration of souls is another binding principle among Hindus. *Karma* pertains to individuals. The individual, however, being determined in his fate by *karma*, also takes part in *samsara*, or the general flow of living creatures who make their way through unending time by a series of reincarnations. The transmigration of souls appears to be a necessary concomitant of the doctrine of *karma*, for it is evident to the Indian mind that recompense for thought and action is not completely determined in this life. But the doctrine of the transmigration of souls also expresses the Hindu belief in the indestructibility of the essence of man, his *atman*, or soul. The doctrine also expresses the Hindu view of the nature of the universe. The cosmos is not conceived as an entity with a beginning and an end. This is a view which is more appropriate to the Judaic religions. Hinduism views the universe as a giant wheel which is endlessly turning, without beginning or ending. So the person, under *karma*, knows no beginning or ending. He is simply one particular within *samsara*, the general flow of things, and his birth-death-rebirth are deemed to be a natural and logical expression of a total view of creation. The concepts of *karma* and of the transmigration of souls constitute only two of the ideas, although they are major in importance, which Hindus generally accept and by which their lives are bound together.

Fifth, caste binds Hindus together in a common faith. Caste is the basic social system of India. Although it is scarcely known in the Vedic period, it did come into power in the time of the Brahmanas, has been criticized and accepted in all later times, but even today caste comprises a significant feature both of Hinduism and of India's life. Fundamentally and historically there are four castes. The *brahmin*, or priestly, caste is at the top of the social order. The functions of this caste are to perform the sacred rituals, to be holy, and to maintain the essential knowledge of the religion. The second caste is composed of the *kshatriyas* who originally were the warriors and also now include those in authority. The third caste, the *vaishyas*, is made up of those who are engaged in commerce, agriculture, and other fairly well-respected occupations. Historically and according to the religious requirements of Hinduism, the fourth caste, the *sudras*, exists to serve the other three castes which in the scheme of things are higher placed. While the general lines of this fourfold caste system still hold in India today, various modifications have occurred to qualify the system greatly. The four basic castes have been further divided into hundreds and even thousands of subcastes. The formally religious character of the castes also has been diminished, so that today the castes and the subcastes are related basically to occupational distinctions, ethnic heritage, and also by regionalism. But without a doubt the general system of caste marks another feature which Hindus hold in common. In fact, many learned commentators on the subject of Hinduism offer caste as the single, most powerful element which binds Hindus together. They say that Hindus may differ and do differ on all of the other elements which comprise the totality of Hinduism, but that on this one feature, that of caste, there can be no exception, for, they say, without the social system of caste all other aspects of the religion can effectively be called into question. Surely, no matter how one settles this special view of caste, no doubt exists for many that caste is a pillar of the religion.

Hinduism, then, is a complex religion that appeals to a very large following. Its success over the centuries can be measured by the plurality of its forms, giving each person and cult a special insight into the nature of reality and a special place in the maintenance of a particular set of truths and practices. Certain elements, such as those discussed, tend to give it at least a nominal or common-denominator basis for being considered as a single religion. The inclusive spirit which has characterized Hinduism over the centuries provides sufficient elasticity of form and belief to assure its continuance in human history.

FOUR

Philosophy

In both the East and the West, as perhaps everywhere, religion and philosophy have always been twin aspects of many mutual concerns. The proper relations between the two have never yet been settled to everyone's satisfaction. They seem to be complementary activities, but at some points the adherents of one or the other see a need to claim that in actuality they are not positively related; in fact, at times and by some they are viewed as opposed. Thus the relations may be deemed problematical. Yet it is not possible to describe Hinduism accurately without taking a look at its philosophical aspects, for Hinduism historically and at present has been identified with philosophy. It has given form to a number of philosophic movements. All of these aspects of Hinduism call for consideration.

Vedism

Philosophy exists in every historical period and form of Hinduism, including the Vedic, although its clearest expression in early times takes place in the Upanishads. In the Vedas, and to a much lesser extent in the Brahmanas, there is at least a latent philosophy, that is, a philosophy which does not pose as such, but which is implicit in the religion of that era. For example, the number of deities says something about the Vedic view of ultimate reality. The Vedas contain animistic and polytheistic representations of deity. They portray nature as the home of divine spirits. In addition, they conceive of a fairly large number of high gods, gods who are not resident in objects, processes, and persons. These high gods, like Agni, Vishnu, Siva, and others, are clearly cosmic beings who cannot be limited to a particular reality. From such a description of the gods in the Vedas, then, it is possible to conclude that the philosophic teaching of this period of Hinduism regarding ultimate reality is pluralistic. There are intimations in the Vedas that there may be one god, two, or even three, who are the final reality. But in the main the Vedas teach pluralism. Monism did not appear in Hinduism as a full-blown doctrine until the Upanishads.

One other idea from the Vedic period, from a large number that are available, may be taken to illustrate Vedic philosophy: the concept of *rita*, or order. This teaching, although probably of older origins, is offered by the Vedas and includes both ethical and cosmic order. It is the forerunner of *karma*. *Rita* suggests the coherence of nature; there is a uniformity that can be detected in all natural phenomena. It also suggests the idea of causality, that no mere happenstance operates in the world. From this notion, moreover, may be derived the interpretation of the meaningfulness of nature, man, and society. That which is regularized must be based upon that which is causally determined, and that which is causally determined must have meaning. From *rita* also is derived the word "right" that pertains to ethical behavior. The right, then, is not a superficial attribute of human action, but is grounded in the very nature of things. The gods, furthermore, are not amoral beings. It is true that in the Vedic period the gods performed in ways that are both good and bad by almost any ethical standard. Yet, taken as a whole, the gods generally stand on the side of the right and are opposed to the wrong. Varuna, for example, is that deity in the Rig Veda who is most seriously responsible for the exercise of *rita*.

Upanishads

The Vedas primarily look to sacrifices and prayer as the effective means to human salvation, while the Brahmanas exalt ritual and other priestly activities. The Upanishads, however, honor *jnana*, or knowledge. They are the first major effort within Hinduism to extol the virtues of knowledge, and in so doing they provide a developed account of philosophical religion. *Jnana*, however, is not only a virtue in itself, an achievement to be sought for its own good. Knowledge has an instrumental character also in that it enables the person with right knowledge to overcome evil. Knowledge is related to salvation. To secure knowledge, moreover, one must fulfill certain conditions. One does not attain to it simply by being active or by wishing strenuously. First, one must be detached, contemplative, quiet, and calm. Second, one must undertake the search for the truth under the guidance of a guru, or teacher. The teacher has two values. He himself has knowledge that is important to the searcher, but he also is by definition an embodiment of the knowledge he professes. Next, one must continue to reflect upon what one has learned until knowledge becomes conviction or is deeply known. Searchers for the truth generally do not directly and immediately apprehend the truth; rather, they must contemplate it again and again in order for its full import to be realized. Correlatively, the nature of genuine knowledge makes this demand upon the searcher. Finally, the searcher reaches an understanding of the relationship he holds to the whole of knowledge. He comes to see that within himself the unity of all knowing is found and expressed. So, according to Upanishadic teaching, knowledge is the source of salvation, a virtue to be sought, but an achievement which is realized only under certain conditions and as a result of careful self-discipline.

The central philosophic teaching of the Upanishads may be taken to be that of Brahma and *atman*. These two concepts are pivotal for the whole later development of Hindu philosophy. Brahma, the true object of all intellectual endeavor, is the one, transcendent, self-existing, principle or deity who is the ground of all phenomenal existence. Philosophically, Brahma represents a form of idealistic monism. Reality, in the view of the Upanishads, is spirit, and spirit is one. The word *brahma* appears to be derived in part from the word for prayer, and in this context the nature of Brahma is holy, that which is most deeply felt. But the word also connotes growth or coming into being. In this connotation Brahma signifies the primal source of all things. Brahma expresses itself and the world comes into existence.

The orthodox sages of Hinduism insist that the Upanishads, like the other *sruti* scriptures, are entirely and literally consistent. But other scholars suggest that the *sruti* scriptures do not necessarily achieve such a degree of consistency. They point to the fact, for example, that Brahma is conceived in the Upanishads generally as impersonal, yet there are some passages that suggest a theistic or personal view of Brahma. Again, Brahma is viewed in the Upanishads essentially as having two kinds of relationship with the created order. First, Brahma is the sum and substance of all things. In this view he is pantheistically conceived. If one asks where Brahma is, the answer is that he is here, there, and everywhere. From this perspective human beings are able to bear a clear and almost observable relationship to Brahma. Second, Brahma is not to be identified with any perception or knowledge of the outer world. That which is observable is the product of Brahma's "breathing," but it is not Brahma. Brahma, from this standpoint, is the ground for all that exists, but Brahma is independent of existence. Brahma is essentially not knowable. Only intimations may be found of his existence, although from a strict standpoint even Brahma's existence involves a category which some Hindu philosophers would claim is not applicable. Any attribute, even that of existence, attached to Brahma is not strictly proper, for attributes in effect seek to limit the limitless.

The concept of the *atman* refers to the nature of the self. The word itself probably originated in the notion of "breath," which was taken to refer to the essence of the person. The person, from a very simple understanding, is alive when he is breathing and is no longer a person when he stops breathing. At any rate, *atman* constitutes the essence of man. Just as Brahma is the essence of the outer world, so *atman* is the essence of the inner self of man, his soul. *Atman*, moreover, is a spiritual or idealistic reality. The body of man, like the outer world in relation to Brahma, is related to man's essence, but generally it does not participate in his essence. A man breathes in his body and gives it its appearance of being real, but ultimately it is *atman* that is truly real.

It is the genius of the Upanishads not only to proffer the concepts of Brahma and *atman* as means of interpreting ultimate reality, but of conjoining them. The Upanishads assert that Brahma and *atman* are not independent or opposed, but that taken together they constitute the true nature of things. Man is composed of the same reality as that upon which the universe rests. Brahma and *atman* are of the same essence. This conclusion, so apparent in the Upanishads, however, does not make man into god. Also, it does not reduce Brahma to human proportions. *Atman* is finite, while Brahma in infinite. Man is able to understand perhaps what Brahma is by understanding his own nature. One of the intimations of Brahma's nature lies in the pathway of self-understanding. But the person must not easily and directly assume that he is Brahma or that through his understanding he has an absolute grasp of the meaning of Brahma.

The foregoing account of Brahma and *atman* is necessarily brief in the light of the present purposes. A fuller account of the nature of the divine is provided in Chapter 5 and a more detailed exposition of the nature of the person is given in Chapter 7. Both themes, moreover, are found in other contexts throughout this book.

Six Schools

The Upanishads represent a high point in the development of Hindu philosophy. It is the hinge of Hindu philosophy in the sense that all later efforts represent doorways to knowledge which find their impetus in the Upanishadic outlook. But the philosophically inclined usually depend upon one of the interpretative schools of Hindu philosophy which arose at times that are later than that of the Upanishads. Traditionally these schools are innumerable and each is distinctive in some regard. But there are six schools of philosophy which are generally regarded as both representative and authoritative. They did not all arise at the same time and they do not all have a final and fixed nature. They have perhaps only one feature in common: they believe that they derive their insights from the *sruti* scriptures and mainly from the Vedas, although their indebtedness to the Upanishads is apparent. These six schools, moreover, are not viewed by Hindu philosophers as being in absolute opposition. Reality, it is claimed, is so complex, Hinduism is so complex, and human thought is so limited in its apprehension of the truth, that all six of these systems are valuable. Each in some sense which is difficult at times to determine complements the others. The six are: Nyaya, Vaiseshika, Sankhya, Yoga, Mimamsa, and Vedanta. Usually, among Hindu scholars, these six are reduced to three: Nyaya and Vaiseshika form one group; Sankhya and Yoga are highly related; and Mimamsa and Vedanta are close to each other. They will be briefly described in these combinations.

Nyaya was originated by Gautama (?450 B.C.-A.D. 100?), who is not the Gautama who founded Buddhism. Born in northern

Bihar, the son of a priest, Gautama spent most of his life in solemn contemplation with his wife and only son. His Nyaya-sutra is an exercise in logic and has gained for him the title of the Aristotle of India. Nyaya is primarily a method of thinking. About A.D. 1200 another logician of note, Gangesa of Mithila, wrote his Tattvacintamani, which became the standard text of the school. In it Gangesa refined the logical methods of Gautama.

The Nyaya school lays heavy emphasis on the modes of thinking. It assumes that right thought cannot be achieved without right thinking. It stresses the basic laws of thought, the ways in which assumptions are made, and the proper way by which conclusions are reached. It makes much of syllogisms and reasoning by analogy. The rules governing the appropriate use of these devices are carefully analyzed and their limits established. At times the Nyaya school is called Tarka-vidya, or the science of reasoning, and at other times Vada-vidya, or the science of discussion.

While the Nyaya school is basically concerned with right reasoning and makes its greatest contribution at this point, it also developed some speculative contributions, although these are probably of lesser value. Originally Nyaya did not deal with god or the gods; the Nyaya-sutra makes only one somewhat oblique reference to deity. Later, however, especially as a result of Saivite influence, the Nyaya school did become theistic. But its main substantive teachings did involve a view of evil and of salvation. Evil in man and the world, according to Nyaya, is due to error. *Apavarga* (deliverance) is brought about, in the spirit of the Upanishads, through *jnana* (right knowledge). Once ignorance is overcome the endless cycles of birth and rebirth will end and the person will attain true happiness. This view of human salvation is the basis for the development of Nyaya's rules of logic, for only by correct thinking is man able to overcome the evil of error. The two most significant features of Nyaya are: *pramana*, the methods by which knowledge is secured, and *prameya*, the object of the methods.

Kanada (about the third century B.C.) is the recognized founder of the Vaiseshika school of Hindu philosophy. Little is known of

Kanada, although it is said that he meditated long and hard, especially about the nature of physical reality. The Nyaya school believes that the analysis advanced by the Vaiseshika school is essentially correct, while the Vaiseshika school says that it arrived at its conclusions through the use of the logical methods of the other school. Thus they are usually grouped together.

Vaiseshika teaches that reality can be divided into atomic essences. Kanada was called an "eater of atoms" and has been regarded as the Heraclitus of India. According to the school, six categories exist fundamentally which regulate all inquiries into reality. First, there is *dravya* (substance). Substance is the one basis for the whole of the universe, although it is further divided into two groups or classes. The one group, termed *paramanu*, consists of earth, water, fire, and air. The other group consists of ether, time, space, soul, and mind. These nine elements with their various attributes constitute the ultimate basis for the whole cosmos. They are either infinitesimal or infinite and equal; thus, the soul and fire have the same standing in this outlook. The *gunas*, or attributes, are the second basic category in Vaiseshika thought. These are numbered usually at twenty-four. They are not basic, as is *dravya*, but they do enjoy an independent existence of their own. Flavor, for example, is an attribute of water as color is of fire. The attribute is not the substance, but it is significant nevertheless. Third, *karma* exists. *Karma* in this context signifies action or motion. This motion is related as are all things to the *dravya*, although it also maintains a separate existence or meaning. *Karma* and the *gunas* bear a similar relation to the basic substances. Fourth, *samanya* (generality) expresses the possibility that the *dravyas* are classifiable and organizable according to types. The pure essences do exist, but they also take the form of specific classes of beings, such as men, trees, and mountains. Although this notion comes close to what Plato taught as ideas, there are differences. Fifth, *visesha* (particularity) is the means by which one member of a class or *samanya* or a universal may be differentiated from others and even from all others. A particular tree, for example, is a member of a universal class termed trees. But a particular tree is itself and no other tree. Each and everything has its own *visesha* even as does each and every group. From this category the school derives its name. Sixth, *samavaya* (necessary relations) also exists. *Samavaya* in a sense is highly similar to a *guna,* for relationship is an attributive characteristic. Yet the Vaiseshika school makes a special category of *samavaya* on the grounds that the relationships between a *dravya* and the *gunas* may vary and do vary, but that at least one essential relationship is required for a *dravya* to be itself. Thus *samavaya* indicates the basic or distinctive relationship that in fact exists between an object and its attributes. To these six categories or "predictables" a seventh was later added, called *abhava* (nonexistence). This category appeared later to be a necessary part of the total system. *Abhava* signifies the absence or negation of an object. It is one thing to make assertions about various existences, but it is necessary to be able to make assertions about absences of existences. The category, however, does not mean the same as nothingness. It simply means that what exists is not necessarily present at a given time or place.

At the start the Vaiseshika school was atheistic and only later did it introduce the idea of god. God is classified under the *dravya* of *atman* or soul. He is not the creator of the *dravya,* although it is claimed that he did have the responsibility for ordering the *dravya* or being the prime agent in creation, although the *dravya* predated his existence.

Another grouping of Hindu philosophic schools is the Sankhya and the Yoga. Sometimes Sankhya is spelled Samkhya. Although they have points in common with the other schools, they are in effect independent but highly related to each other. The Sankhya is probably very old, although it is not very popular in recent times. Some scholars have traced its origins directly to the Upanishads, but that tie is too tenuous to make the claim valid. Traditionally the founder of Sankhya is Kapila (*ca.* 500 B.C.), who was the son of a *rishi,* or inspired seer, although it was his mother, Devahuti, who taught him the basic elements of philosophy. He lived the second half of his life on a small island, the Sagar, at the mouth of the Ganges. Whatever he taught is not presently available, since the Sankhya-sutra which presumably is his contribution dates only to about the fifteenth century A.D. It is said, however, to contain the elements of Kapila's original teachings. Probably the earliest work which is authoritative, the Sankhya-karika, was written by Isvarakrishna in about the fifth century A.D. This work is such a clear exposition of the doctrines of Sankhya that it has been widely praised as perhaps the best work of its kind in Indian philosophy.

The most fundamental teaching of the Sankhya school consists of a dualism: *purusha* (spirit) and *prakriti* (matter). The Nyaya-Vaiseshika school taught that the world consists of a large number of atoms or irreducible substances. Sankhya, on the other hand, refers all existence ultimately to a basic dualism. Only two irreducible elements, mind and nature, really exist. These account for everything. *Purusha,* unlike *prakriti,* is passive and motionless spirit. Although it is everywhere and exists in all time, it is changeless. *Prakriti,* however, is the sole causal agent in the universe, the basis for all change, and the former of all that is physical. *Prakriti* does not cause or control *purusha.* But all else, including space and time, are bound by it. These two principles, then, related yet unrelated, constitute the uncompromising dualism of the San-khya school.

Change is recognized to be basic to the universe. But something cannot be created from nothing. Whatever exists has always existed, although different forms are possible. Change, moreover, appears as evolution, that is, there is some direction or purpose evident in change. This evolution, however, is not Darwinian in concept, assuming that change is purposefully directed in a seemingly unending way and always toward greater complexity. Some degree of such change is evident to the Sankhyan philosophers. But change of this nature does not pertain to groups and classes of objects; only the individual rather than the species evolves. Again, evolution is not unending but is cyclical; it has a periodicity.

The purpose of change, furthermore, is not of high sentiency; it is less evident and less likely to be maintained, for the *prakriti* has a natural tendency to revert to itself. All change or evolution tends to suffer from dissolution, otherwise it would be endless in its direction.

Purusha and *prakriti,* the two dualistically conceived realities, are the first two in a series of twenty-five *tattvas* (categories), but the others are thought to be the result of the interrelations between the first two.

The Sankhya school is not basically theistic. While it does not deny the existence of a personal deity, it finds no place for such a being. Also, it rejects the importance of Vedic sacrifices, although it holds the Vedas as part of the *sruti* scriptures. The notion of suffering, perhaps received as a Buddhist influence, is strong in Sankhya, although the idea of extreme asceticism or withdrawal from the world also is rejected.

Yoga, a well-known term in the West as well as the East, is another of the six orthodox schools of Hindu philosophy. In essence it is a form of physical and mental exercises which are aimed at the improvement of life for the *yogi,* or practitioner. One who is well advanced in this kind of self-discipline is commonly called a *yogarudha.* Yoga consists of ascetic practices some of which are even pre-Aryan in their origin. In its earlier forms it possesses elements of a magic ritualism which have continued even to the present. Even today factors of occultism and of sorcery are found within some aspects of it.

Hindu tradition avers that Yoga's originator was Yajnavalkya, an early sage, whose ideas were made more systematic by Patanjali in his Yoga-sutra. The development of the school's philosophy, however, has not been overly systematic, and elements of Yoga practice can be found in many Hindu systems of contemplation that do not claim to be a part of the school.

Yoga and Sankhya are related. Followers of Yoga assert that Sankhya supplies the metaphysical basis for them. They are ready to affirm the highly sophisticated tenets of the Sankhya philosophy.

On the other hand, the followers of Sankhya believe that Yoga appropriately provides them with a practical expression for their more intellectual outreach. Yoga thinkers, however, usually add one more *tattva* to Sankhya's twenty-five. It is the belief in Isvara, or god. Isvara is a relatively late importation into the system and does not signify a creator of the universe or a *tattva* which is independent of the others. He is mainly an object for contemplation, a useful means for personalizing the ascetic exercises. Portions of Patanjali's Yoga-sutra which allude to Isvara appear to be rather unconnected with the rest of the work and may have been inserted into the document at a time when the doctrine became popular.

No single form of Yoga exists; rather, a very large number are available, each being based upon the goals that are sought and the means that are employed. Probably the most important systems are: *karma-yoga,* or salvation through works; *bhakti-yoga,* or salvation through faith; *jnana-yoga,* or salvation through knowledge; *mantra-yoga,* or salvation through the use of *mantras* or spells; *laya-yoga,* or salvation through the stimulation of the *chakras* or subtle centers of the body; *hatha-yoga,* or salvation through physical culture or exercises; and *raja-yoga,* or salvation by the use of spiritual development. Each of these forms of Yoga also consists of a particular number of *bhumi,* or stages by which the *yogi* advances to his goal. The number of stages, for example, are: in *bhakti-yoga,* nine; in *laya-yoga,* ten; in *raja-yoga,* fifteen; and in *hatha-yoga,* eight.

Hatha-yoga may be viewed as the prototype of the other forms and it is probably the most popular today. Sometimes persons who speak of Yoga think of only this one form. Its primary object is the improvement of the well-being of the body with its concomitant benefits to the body's functions, including mental benefits. Basically it is dualistic in outlook. *Ha* in *hatha* is thought to refer to the sun and *tha* is said to refer to the moon. The sun and the moon symbolize the two principles that are apparent in every human being. This polarity is expressed in *hatha-yoga* in reference to the person: two breaths are taken into the body through two nostrils, every person has two genders at work within him, and the need for the person to control the body in the interests of the spirit.

Hatha-yoga calls upon its devotees to follow eight *bhumi* or stages in order to attain to the final goal. First, *yama,* or restraint or control of the external activities; sexual continence is thus assumed to be helpful, and causing no physical harm to others is deemed a virtue. Second, *niyama,* or internal control, follows upon the first stage. Internal control means that the person who practices *hatha-yoga* must seek to control his inner activism, his constant striving. He should become quiet and contemplative, so that his essential self may rise to the surface. Third, *asanas,* or bodily postures. These are viewed as necessary disciplines in order that the body may be made to serve the individual and not contrariwise. Fourth, *pranayama,* or breath control, which is thought of as an extension, although more difficult and therefore more profitable, than the bodily exercises. Fifth, *pratyahara,* or control of the senses. The senses are the gateways to the self and their control is necessary in the ascent to fulfillment. Sixth, *dharana,* or meditation, signifies the step, when the body has come under complete discipline, which is purely mental and therefore higher. Seventh, *dhyana,* or contemplation, connotes greater freedom mentally and offers the prospect of a basic spiritual creativity. Finally, *samadhi,* or a form of superconsciousness in which the person is released from all restraints of the body and mind and is able to attain complete fulfillment. The final stage has been said to be related to the state of blessedness as taught by Gautama, the founder of Buddhism, and to *nirvana,* another Buddhist term for the same condition. In *nirvana* the self is freed from itself, the person is enlightened, he has achieved his salvation.

The third and final set of schools of Hindu philosophy are the Mimamsa and the Vedanta. The Mimamsa differs from the Vedanta in that it lays primary stress upon the means of knowing, especially by analyzing literature and words, while the Vedanta is clearly more speculative, being primarily concerned with substantive issues in philosophy. Yet, as with the other combinations of schools, these two bear a positive relationship to each other. Mimamsa aids Vedanta in the clarification of meanings. Vedanta provides content to the linguistic work of Mimamsa.

Mimamsa, like the other schools, is difficult to date in its origins. It is said to have come into being with Jaimini, who in turn was a disciple of Badarayana. Jaimini may have lived as early as 400 B.C., although some scholars place him at about 200 B.C. His Mimamsa-sutra, the chief source for this school, however, may have been recorded about A.D. 200.

Mimamsa differs from the other philosophic schools in that it greatly relies upon the Vedas as the most authoritative source of knowledge. The other schools vary in their dependence on the Vedas, but Mimamsa is almost completely centered in them. Mimamsa does recognize also the other *sruti* scriptures, the Brahmanas and the Upanishads, but its first reliance is upon the Vedas. Mimamsa also is concerned with the proper means of interpreting the Vedas. The followers of this school believe that revelation comes to man through words. Words in themselves do not constitute the revelation but, rather, reflect the revelation. The object in Mimamsa, then, is to study those devices by which the words can be separated from the deposit of revelation, to use words, as they have been employed in the Vedas, to express the revelation, and to seek to harmonize the seeming variations within the Vedas, so that coherent truth may be found and communicated. In this regard, Mimamsa is not particularly at odds with the other systems of philosophy. It chiefly wishes for clarity in the meaningfulness of essential Hinduism. It believes, furthermore, that knowledge in itself is valuable, but it cannot lead to salvation. Knowledge without right action is fruitless. Right action involves the proper performance of the Hindu ceremonies. By engaging in ceremonialism the believer is able to initiate those benefits which bring advantages to the person even in the future life. *Dharma* (right action) is the rule for all life.

Mimamsa is sometimes called Purva-Mimamsa, or early Mimamsa, to distinguish it from the Vedanta school which at times is referred to as Uttara-Mimamsa, or later Mimamsa. The straight reference to Vedanta, however, is the more general and popular. Traditionally Vedanta is said to have been originated by Badarayana who lived sometime before the Christian era. His Vedantasutra is a basic source for this school, although some parts of his *sutra* are difficult to understand. Some scholars identify him with Jaimini, who is presumed to be the founder of Mimamsa, while others think that he may have been a compiler of the Vedas and the Mahabharata.

Vedanta is the high point of the Vedas, as the name implies, and this school recognizes the Vedas as *sruti,* or revealed. Yet Vedanta in its various forms relies most heavily upon the Upanishads for its inspiration and guidance. Vedanta teaches that man finds his salvation not in *moksha* (release) but by becoming a *jivan-mukta* (fully realized person). The person is one with Brahma, the most real, and by seeking true knowledge the individual is able to overcome his errors and limits and become one with the real. Knowledge, however, is not a simple product of the human mind, but is a state of being which is achieved through intuition and inspiration, especially as these are made available by *rishis* (sages).

The Vedanta school, however, is divided into two subsections. One of these, Advaita, maintains a strict monism, believing that Brahma is a pantheistic reality who overcomes all particularity. The other, Dvaita, is essentially but by varying degrees dualistic, asserting that man and his world are in some sense real and apart from Brahma.

Advaita is uncompromisingly monistic in its outlook. It asserts that reality is one, referring to one of the *mahavakyas,* or great sayings, of the Upanishads, "one essence and no other." Brahma is that one essence. Advaita believes that references in the other schools and beyond them in Hinduism to multiple realities must be taken as allegorical rather than literal. Advaita asserts that when the Sankhya school, for example, speaks of *purusha* (spirit) and *prakriti* (matter) as the two basic realities, it fails to appreciate that these are merely two aspects of the one basic reality and that Brahma is that reality. The phenomenal world does appear to have an independent existence, according to Advaita, but actually this appearance is a consequence of *maya* (illusion). Maya is a powerful force in human perceptions; it is like a huge net or veil which obscures man's vision of the truly real. Intuitive vision, such as that advocated in Advaita, frees man from *maya,* and he is then able to appreciate the oneness of things. *Maya* accounts for man's inherent tendency to believe in *avachchheda* (separateness), by which he concludes that things do exist apart from Brahma. True knowledge, however, indicates that Brahma is the only reality and that persons are a part of Brahma. The *paramatman,* or supreme soul, and the *jivatman,* or the individual soul, are one.

Advaita philosophy was advocated by Sankara (A.D. 788-838), who was born in Kaladi and grew up in what is now Travancore. His father, a brahmin, died when Sankara was still a child and it was his mother who reared him and gave him a taste for philosophy. Although he was pledged by his mother to marry, he finally was able to persuade her to permit him to become a *sannyasin,* or one who devotes himself wholly to *moksha* (salvation). Sankara in his quest for salvation studied under the guru Govindapada, who in turn had studied under an even more famous philosopher, Gaudapada. Sankara was an apt pupil and in time became famous not only for his knowledge but also for his great debating skills. He traveled extensively, both teaching and learning, until his death in the village of Kedarnath, near the Himalayas.

Sankara taught the uncompromising monism of Advaita. In so doing he was principally a commentator who brought a finely honed and critical mind to the task of expounding a system of thought. He was not an originator. He took philosophic elements which were everywhere around him in his time and wove them into a meaningful fabric. In this regard he was undoubtedly indebted to both Buddhism and Islam for some of his ideas as well as the Upanishadic tradition. Sankara, however, in many respects was a traditionalist in Hinduism. He believed strictly in caste and thought that the *sudras,* members of the agricultural and artisan caste, for example, should not be permitted to read the Vedas. He himself, despite his Advaita teachings, was able to worship idols and composed hymns to Vishnu, Siva, Parvati, and others, in addition to his avowal of the primacy of Brahma. In Sankara, however, Advaita Vedantism had a major intellectual advocate.

The Dvaita subsection of the Vedanta school of orthodox Hindu philosophy has had a number of able expositors, but among them two leading thinkers may be reviewed here as providing a sound account of Dvaita: Ramanuja and Madhva.

Ramanuja (?A.D. 1017-1137?) was born near Madras, the grandson of a leader of the Vaishnava sect in south India. Early he studied under a famed Advaita philosopher, Yadava-prakasa. His father died when Ramanuja was young; a marriage did not work out and he became despondent. He decided to become a holy man and after traveling widely in northern India he settled in Drirangam in southern India. He concentrated upon the sacred Vedas and in time wrote commentaries on them and on other Hindu works. He belonged to the Vaishnavite sect even as Sankara was a member of the Saivites. He was basically intuitive in his philosophic activities, while Sankara was rationalistic. Ramanuja was disturbed by many aspects of the popular religion of his day. He deplored the ignorance of the people which was capitalized upon by the avariciousness of the brahmins. Although he believed in the caste system, Ramanuja was a strong advocate of the worth of women. He sought the social and religious equality of men and women, especially through education, of which, again, he was a persistent advocate.

Philosophically Ramanuja taught that both Brahma and the non-Brahma are real. He believed that there is only one deity who goes by several names, including Brahma, Vishnu, and Isvara. Brahma existed before the world and is the creator of all existence. He is the first cause. Nothing exists that has not been brought into existence by Brahma. Brahma, moreover, is spiritual in nature, while the created world is *achit* (unconscious). Materiality exists truly and is not *maya* (illusion), but it is dependent in creation and continually upon Brahma (spirit). Nothing that has been created can resist Brahma, for to be supreme his will must be done. But Brahma takes pity on his creation, including human beings, and at times becomes incarnate in various forms, his incarnation in the god Rama being the finest expression of his nature and his love for mankind.

Ramanuja also taught the reality of the *jiva,* or human soul. The soul is an *amsa,* or fragment, of Brahma. But the soul is not totally Brahma; it is merely a particle. The individual soul is in fact dependent, as is all else, upon Brahma, but also maintains its own identity. Even at such time as the individual soul may be reunited with Brahma, it still retains its distinct reality. Obviously in Ramanuja's philosophy the Brahma and the non-Brahma are two kinds of reality. Thus his thought is sometimes called *visishiadvaita,* or a qualified nondualism. Although god is truly supreme in Ramanuja's thought, he or Brahma is not pantheistically conceived; all that is non-Brahma also truly exists.

Sankara taught that reality has a fundamental unity, while Ramanuja taught that a degree of separateness exists between the creator and the creation. Madhva (A.D. 1197-1280) taught that the soul is thoroughly divorced from Brahma, a more pronounced *dvaita* or dualistic doctrine. Madhva, born in a village near Mangalore of brahmin parents, took an early interest in learning and was said to have mastered the Vedas while a child. Early he took to teaching and preaching, going about his area to stimulate interest in the worship of Vishnu. He became convinced that Advaita philosophy was in error. He visited some of Sankara's centers of acceptance, such as Srinagar where Sankara had established a *math* (monastery), and brought his message of dualism. In Ramesvaram he entered into debate and there wrote a commentary which has been held in high regard by his disciples. He not only attacked the Advaita philosophy of Sankara, but also learned

Persian so that he could hold critical discourses with Muslim leaders, seeking to convince them of their errors. Finally he returned to his birthplace, Udipi. There he taught and secured many disciples. In time a Hindu sect came into being centered on Madhva and his teachings. Madhva himself was revered by his followers, who believed that he possessed supernatural powers. They, for example, believed that he had walked upon the waters, had fed them generously with a few loaves, and that he had stilled the stormy seas at a word. Some scholars see in this reverence as well as in his teachings the influence of Christian teachings.

Madhva believed, like Sankara and Ramanuja, in the supremacy of Brahma. Brahma exists and is the prime cause of the world and of human beings. Yet the *jiva,* or soul, of persons is not a fragment of the divine essence. The soul consists of its own essence, independent of Brahma. So there are two entities that are in effect supreme. The individual's soul maintains itself through all time. It is not lost within Brahma upon its emancipation. If reality can properly be graded, then the soul is on a lower level than Brahma. Brahma is perfect; the soul admittedly in Madhva's thought is imperfect. But the soul, though imperfect, is necessarily real and independently existing from Brahma.

The Madhvan sect, however, practices religion in a way which is somewhat different from the philosophic teachings of its founder. The Hinduism of the Madhvan sect recognizes, for example, the legitimacy of worshiping Vishnu. Some also worship Siva. They believe that Vishnu's son, Vayu, is an especially effective agent of the deity in aiding mankind in its search for *moksha,* or ultimate release. They also believe that Madhva was an incarnation of Vayu and was divinely commissioned to teach his views of the falsity of the Advaita philosophy. Madhva himself taught a stricter form of Hinduism than his followers later practiced. He, for instance, taught that bloody sacrifices should be abandoned in favor of the use of dough and that temple prostitutes were unworthy of the temple. His followers, however, later reintroduced many of the more traditional practices of Hinduism. Madhva remains as an exemplar of the Dvaita philosophy of the Vedanta school.

These six schools are sometimes called *shad-darsana,* or six views of philosophy. Obviously they are not all the same either in general outlook or in their particulars. But many Hindus aver that they are six ways by which limited men, although they often were uncommonly inspired, have seen ultimate reality. Loyal Hindus do not necessarily consider the six systems to be entirely in opposition, especially in an emotionally derived or combatant sense. Rather, they are six views of the nature of truth or reality which suit the needs of those who are intellectually inclined. The six all claim in varying degrees to be based upon the *sruti* scriptures: the Vedas, the Brahmanas, and the Upanishads. In general they accept the Indian caste system as normative and they accept such basic Hindu doctrines as *karma* (causality) and the transmigration of souls. Their teachings are often embodied in commentaries on the *sruti* scriptures. These commentaries mainly are *sutras,* or writings with teachings in the form of aphorisms. Indeed, the six schools hold many concepts in common, although the exact meaning that is assigned to them within the individual schools varies. Chiefly, too, the schools are *astika,* or believing, in contrast to the *nastika* philosophers, who basically were deniers. The six affirm, especially in their later forms, the existence of a supreme being. Most often that being is Brahma. The systems, moreover, are principally concerned with doctrines of god and man to the exclusion of many other topics which would be considered by modern philosophers, especially in the Western tradition, to comprise a complete or systematic philosophy. In that sense these six schools may be termed philosophies of religion rather than philosophies as such. To a large degree they have remained primarily as philosophies, permeating much of the intellectual life of India over the centuries. In some instances, however, they have been combined in sectarian movements which have compromised to some extent with popular Hinduism, each oftentimes maintaining their separate meanings and values. Although the six schools developed within the mainstream of Hinduism's history, they also have been influenced by systems outside that faith, such as Jainism, Buddhism, Islam, and Christianity. But they stand today as six *darsanas,* or views, of Hinduism's insights into the nature of ultimate reality.

Philosophic Hinduism is only one strand of the religion, yet it illustrates that the religion possesses intellectual power. It has sought to harness intelligence in the service of faith and to an astonishing degree has succeeded by providing its followers with systems of reasoning that are established upon the foundations of essentially religious questions or problems. Hinduism is more than an intellectual exercise resulting in a set of philosophies, but its philosophic contributions are of major standing.

FIVE

The Gods

Quite possibly the core of a religion is what it believes to be the nature of the divine. Usually the divine is granted the term *god,* although god within a particular religion may have more than one referent. But man regularly and perhaps even universally is able to distinguish between himself and the world around him and to see in realities that are not himself those forces and values which he holds in awe, which to him are not himself and over which he does not have complete control. Sometimes this realm beyond man is sensed to be largely natural and is related to the various processes of life itself which seem to maintain themselves without man's conscious control. But at other times these factors are highly personal and even moral, relating directly to man in his innermost mind and emotions, making requirements of him in his behavior which are deemed by him and by others to be obligations. Even when these obligations appear to be set in opposition to what man thinks he naturally wishes to do and appear to be expressions of a countermanding and limiting conscience, man nevertheless chooses to obey the other rather than self. All of these elements, and others, are found within Hinduism, which make important an understanding of the divine as it takes form within that religion.

Verbal formulations of the nature of the divine in Hinduism show great variation and indicate, beyond any other attribute, that poetic and mythological activities represent the most used literary devices to express the ineffable. With certain exceptions, those which pertain to the stricter philosophic efforts, the Hindu mind looks upon ideas of the divine in allegorical rather than literal terms. Words, concepts, stories, and other forms of expression are not viewed as scientific formulations to be tested in a laboratory but, rather, are creative fancies with some basis in human experience. So mythology is as highly developed in the literature of Hinduism as in any religion. A great part of the sacred scriptures tell religious truths in story form. They relate through personages the heroic events of the past, the ways in which man and his gods have been related, the forces of evil that have been brought under control with the help of the gods, the manner in which the cosmos was formed and continues to exist, and other matters that fall within the scope of Hinduism. These myths have been gathered from many early tribes in India and show the influence of foreign peoples as well. They do not make a harmonious whole, moreover, but relate the mythopoetic efforts of various peoples at divers times to account for their experience with the divine.

Cosmology

In accounting for the outer world of man, the universe, Hinduism nonsystematically holds to a particular world-view, or cosmology. Generally speaking, cosmology has two parts: cosmogony, or the nature of creation, and cosmography, a description of the universe after creation. As might be expected, there are several versions in Hinduism as to how the universe was created. A popular account

from the Rig Veda says that at the beginning there was neither
existence nor nonexistence, that the worlds, the sky, and death had
not been established. All was indistinguishable water. At this time
the first cause, who is eternal and variously named, created the
Hiranya-garbha, or golden womb. This golden cosmic egg floated
on the indistinguishable waters. Creation was at work. The golden
egg then divided itself into two parts. The top half of gold became
the heavens, while the silver lower half (notice the change in
metal!) formed the earth. From the various elements in the lower
half the rest of the world was formed: the fluids formed the seas,
the veins the rivers, the outer membrane the mountains, the inner
membranes the clouds and mists. In later times this creation
process, which has been open to many variations in the telling,
was ascribed ultimately to Brahma, the truly transcendent deity
of the Upanishadic period and later. Some schools of orthodox
Hindu philosophy, such as the Sankhya, as described in the previous chapter, had difficulty locating a single and personal source
of responsibility for creation. Thus two eternal elements, *purusha*
(spirit) and *prakriti* (matter) are involved, although the material
world is usually said to have evolved or was made through the
agency of *prakriti.* In early accounts, however, the creation is so
momentous and difficult a task as to engage the actions of a number of deities. So Vishnu made fast the world by pegs, Savriti by
bonds, while Brihaspati held up the ends. At other times it is said
that Brahma was aided by such gods as Prajapati, Purusha, Visva-
karman, Yama, and Yami.

Hinduism's cosmography is not entirely clear and simple, although its general outlines are available, both from the *sruti* and
the *smriti* scriptures and some of the philosophic texts. The creation is composed of three fundamental zones, a zone commonly
being called *loka* (locality). These zones are further divided into
twenty-one *lokas,* although the exact placing of these is at times
obscure. The first major zone is the *loka,* the designation holding
for both the general system and for the first zone. The first *loka*
is the home of the gods; it is heaven. Here the gods make their

dwelling, and their lives are spent within it. At its core is Mount Meru, which is said to tower over all creation. Made of pure gold, it is the pivot around which all creation moves.

In addition to the doctrine of the transmigration of souls, Hinduism also provides for a paradise for human beings and it is located in the first and highest *loka*. Paradise, in the Hindu tradition, is a place of the most satisfying pleasure. It offers the good person a luxurious living in which he walks among green fields, lives in palaces, listens to sweet music, enjoys only the best food, has his desires sated by appealing *apsaras,* or attractive nymphs, and in general enjoys his senses.

The second major zone is the *tala,* or place which constitutes the subterranean regions of the universe. Here dwell the chthonian beings, those deities and spirits that inhabit the underworld. Within it live demons, titans, and giants that cause so much human misery. Within the *tala* also burns a fire which at the end of time will burn up the whole universe. The *tala* is not a human habitation; it is the realm of evil forces and personalities that are often described in terms of their physical deformities as well.

Naraka, or hell, is the third major *loka* in the Hindu cosmography. Like the other localities it consists of a number of subdivisions. One division contains those that are childless (showing the value of children), another is reserved for those who are awaiting reincarnation. Another division is the place where torments originate for the departed, while yet another is a bottomless pit from whence one can have no hope of being reborn again, but must suffer unending pain.

The creation exists in time, and for the Hindu the course of events is definitely proscribed. The gods exist in limited time periods. These are termed a *kalpa,* or aeon. Man, on the other hand, while being related to the divine requirements of time, also exists within *yurgas,* or ages. Human history, then, is the story of the *yurgas.* Four *yurgas* govern human time. They have two essential attributes. First, each succeeding age is briefer in time than the preceding ones. Second, each age is worse than the preceeding ones in creative and ethical achievement. *Krita-yurga,* the first age, is the idyllic period of man's existence. All men are members of a single caste and brotherhood is everywhere practiced. All men revere the Vedas and worship only the one, true god. Men also are highly moral, practicing no hatred or crime, and they live for four thousand years. Being physical and intellectual giants, they are able to fulfill all their desires, even so far as having children merely through wishing.

In the second *yurga,* the *treta-yurga,* the quality of this stage decreases by one-fourth. Men live for a mere three thousand years and have offspring by touch. Four Vedas replace the one, and mankind needs rituals to express religion. While the chief virtue of this age is knowledge, instead of pure spirituality, men also are more self-centered in their lives, giving way to various kinds of evils, including the need to be rewarded for one's work.

In the *dvapara-yurga,* or third age of mankind, righteousness is only one-half of the first stage. Men live only two thousand years; children come through copulation, although sexual relations are characterized by the limits of the law and by personal purity. The family is significant. The Puranas, a set of scriptures, are the guides of the age, and sacrifice is the main religious expression. Natural calamities befall men and diseases become his lot. Truth and duty are not held in high regard and the moral deterioration of this age requires each man to look to his own satisfactions.

The fourth and present age of mankind is termed the *kali-yurga.* By now the first three ages have passed. Some Hindu scholars think that they can date the start of this age (3102 B.C.) and believe that about 500,000 years yet remain in it. At its close the world will be destroyed by fire and flood. Further deterioration has taken place and the creative and moral attributes of this age are only one-tenth of the first. Men's lives are greatly shortened; few live to be a hundred years old. Sexual relations are disturbed. Homosexuality is practiced and permitted, women of virtue are difficult to find, men seek relationships outside of marriage. Sexuality and materiality are the twin concerns of the people in this age. Diseases also are rampant, including mental problems. Persons excel in the baser attributes of lying, stealing, being dishonest, killing. Truly the course of historical development from a qualitative standpoint is not positive; collective human growth through the ages is downward. Such a framework for man's four-staged life provides a basis for the pessimism which is widely thought to be a fundamental characteristic of Hindu teachings and life.

The four *yurgas,* however, possess certain common features. Each has a distinctive color: white for the first, red for the second, yellow for the third, and black for the present *yurga.* Also, each is introduced by a period of time, called its *samdhya,* or morning twilight, in which the promise of the age is especially bright. Similarly, each age closes with a period, called *samdhyamsa* or evening twilight, in which an Indian-summer-like resurgence takes place.

The four *yurgas* taken together comprise a *maha-yurga,* or great *yurga.* One thousand of these make an *ardha-kalpa,* which in turn is simply either one day or one night in the life of Brahma. A *kalpa* consists of two *ardha-kalpas,* which is calculated to be a night and a day of Brahma. A *kalpa* is said to consist of over eight billion human years. Thus the *yurgas* of man, like man himself, undergo the everlasting cycle of birth, death, and rebirth.

Believers

Theologically, Hindu thought consists of both *nastikas* (deniers) and *astikas* (believers). While the affirmers far outnumber those who deny, it is well to note that Hinduism has a long and respected tradition in which atheism has been held to be the true view of things. Ajita (d. 480 B.C.), for example, is illustrative of those who deny. He taught that the universe, including man, is composed of four elements: water, air, fire, and earth. Only the senses are the doorway to knowledge, but reason under the service of the emotions persistently distorts sense knowledge and, therefore, all human knowledge is suspect. Nothing finally makes any difference.

Man does not survive death and the cycle of birth-death-rebirth is an illusion. The body upon death dissolves and is no more. The human spirit does not survive the body. Ethical judgments are not valid and one may follow pleasure as a norm for conduct or not, according to one's pleasure. Good and evil are not punished, for *karma* (retribution) is denied. Thus, as in the example of Ajita, the believing function of man is lacking in objective validation.

But Hindus in the main have been *astikas* (believers). In fact, they have been capable of believing in as many or more divine realities than any peoples known to students of history. In Hinduism almost every form of belief in divine beings can be found. Often there is little if any effort to harmonize these various and diverse beliefs. Taken together, especially from an allegorical and poetic viewpoint, they comprise a very rich historic deposit of affirmation of the existence of the divine in human affairs. The Rig Veda, for example, refers to the number of gods as thirty-three, a symbolic number, who are said to reign over the three *lokas*. Yet the Rig Veda actually refers to more than that sacred number. The number elsewhere is raised to 333, then to 3,333, and so on until the assertion is made that more than three million deities exist. By extension it has been said that every Hindu has a counterpart in a deity. This, obviously, is *astika,* or believing. The beliefs range from the animism of the Vedas to the superpersonal monism of the Upanishads, and no satisfying set of categories exists that adequately can make logical order out of the diversity of Hindu belief.

Some of the deities found in Hinduism were taken over from the pre-Vedic period and belonged originally to early tribes. Khandoba, for example, is such a deity. He was recognized in southern and western India in very early times and is still worshiped by many today. One account says that in early times the people were troubled by a giant, Manimalla, who went about the earth harming and killing the faithful. But Khandoba at the request of the people engaged the giant in a six-day battle, destroying him.

Traditionally the god was said to have the head of a dog and even today canine features are included in his worship, such as barking by temple attendants at annual festivals.

Other deities found in Hinduism have been borrowed from foreign sources. Dyaus is such an example. Dyaus is the cognate deity to the Greek Zeus whose worship was known to the Aryans before they invaded India. Dyaus often represents the father figure among the Hindu gods in contrast to Prithivi, the earth-mother. Sometimes she is called Bhumi or earth or Urvi or broad and is pictured in the Vedas as a cow. The Vedas celebrate the two as the father and the mother of the universe. Ushas, the goddess of the dawn who figures prominently in the Rig Veda, is Dyaus's daughter.

Vedic Deities

The Vedic period offers the greatest number and assortment of deities. These in the main represent various objects and forces in nature. Nature worship was widespread, although evidence suggests that elaborate idolatry and ritualism are minimal. The early Hindus worshiped almost everything that was observed and the list would include, among others: trees, pools, stones, the sky, moon, planets, men, birds, departed ancestors, demons, nymphs, snakes, cows, monkeys, rivers. But the Vedic period also was one of polytheism, the belief in many gods. These gods commonly are not confined to revered objects, but have an existence in the heavens or, in other words, possess a nature of a transcendental dimension. Among the principal gods of this period are Aditi, a mother deity, and her children, the Adityas; Agni, god of fire; Aryaman, god of the souls of the dead; the Asvins, twin gods of the heavens; the Maruts, gods of the storms; Mitra, god of light; Parjanya, god of the rain; Rudra, chief of the storm gods; Saranyu, mother of the Asvins; Surya, god of the sun; Varuna, god of the water; Vayu, god of the wind; Vivasvat, an aspect of the sun god; and Yama, god of death. These deities, along with some others, make up the pantheon of the Vedic era. As is obvious from their naming, each god possessed a particular function, although some of the gods shared in some of the functions. Each is identified with some aspect of nature or human life and is worshiped as a sign of reverence for the successful maintenance of this function in human life and the universe.

Each of the gods has a complex nature. A description of two gods, Rudra and Yama, may be taken as illustrative of the larger number. Rudra, chief of the storm gods, is described in the Brahmanas as having wept greatly upon his birth because he had been given no name. Thus the name Rudra means "weeper." He is pictured as essentially a destructive deity, riding a wild boar about the skies and earth, spreading havoc and even disease. He is the father of the minor storm gods, the Maruts. As Hindu mythology evolved, Rudra became Siva, a very important deity, although generally he grew into the destructive aspect of Siva only.

Yama is a Rig Veda deity who is the judge and punisher of the dead. It is claimed that originally he was a human being who succeeded in finding his way into divinity and was consequently deified. Another claim is that he was the son of the sun god Vivasvat. Yama, green in color, with red clothing and a deformed leg, holds forth in his palace in the netherworld. There souls are brought to him and he passes judgment upon them for their actions while alive. The good are then sent to the higher *lokas,* while the bad are sent to the lower ones. Yama also has a twin sister, Yami.

Div is the term used to designate the major deities in the Vedic period and beyond. It means "shine," for the principal gods were thought to be resplendent in their nature. The tales that are told about them indicate that they have a majesty which connotes their august stature. But there are lesser gods in Hinduism, many of them, and these usually are called *devata,* or godlings. The even more minor deities—of which there are even a larger number, associated with village worship—are termed *grama-devata,* or gods of inferior status. The worship of idols in Hinduism also is extensive.

In general Hindus recognize the existence of many gods even though they individually may have chosen one (or a few) as their special patron. It is to this patron-god that they most often pray and invoke the divine presence. This god for the person, then, is considered the supreme deity even though it is known that in various times and circumstances the patron-god may be exchanged for one (or others) who is considered to be most able to answer human need. Members of Hindu sects center their worship on the sect deity.

At times, however, the gods may be thought of in combinations. For example, in the *panchayatana* ritual (the ritual of the five abodes) five deities are invoked. Places are marked on the floor or objects are placed representing the five deities, who are: Ganesa, Vishnu, Siva, Durga, and Surya. At other times the gods are worshiped in pairs. Thus, in early Hinduism there were such combinations as Dyavaprithivi, a conjoined form for Dyaus, sky, and Prithivi, earth; Mitravarunau, for Mitra and Varuna; Indravishnu, for Indra and Vishnu; and Indragni, for Indra and Agni. Sometimes in later Hinduism as a consequence of the uniting of two sects, each with its own deity, a twin deity was recognized and worshiped. The gods also are grouped into threes. For example, the three *lokas* are believed to be ruled over by three deities: Savitri, the sun; Indra, the heavens; and Agni, fire. Sometimes in place of these three, three others are named: Surya, the sun; Vayu, the wind; and Agni, fire.

The Trimurti

All of these combinations of deities, however, became of lesser importance when the *trimurti,* or three forms of later Hinduism, came into being. These are Brahma, the creator; Vishnu, the sustainer; and Siva, the destroyer. These three are the truly great gods of Hinduism. They take precedence in the minds of most Hindus as far transcending the lesser gods in appeal and in importance. A brief description of each of the three is in order.

Brahma was not known in the Vedic period. He came into prominence with the Upanishads and later was assigned one of the most significant places in the *trimurti*. The description of Brahma in the Upanishads became normative for later considerations of his nature and work, although variant doctrines of Brahma make the task of interpreting him not easy. Today Brahma, unlike the other gods in the triad, is not widely worshiped. There are only two temples in India dedicated to him and one bathing *ghat,* or bathing place, with gently sloping steps into the water.

By and large Brahma is considered as impersonal, that is, he is spoken of in the neuter form. He is believed to be the one supreme reality concerning whom no humanly conceived terms are adequate. To name him is to limit him. All designations are partial and, therefore, inadequate to a full and proper understanding of him. Hindu tradition says that he created the universe and then undertook the *asvamedha* (horse sacrifice) at Bithur, at the site of the *ghat,* and then ascended into the first *loka,* but on his way he left the toe-pin of his wooden shoes, which became lodged in one of the *ghat's* steps. This pin is worshiped today. But it is also said to be his only discrete sign that he is indeed existent.

Belief in the impersonal Brahma also means that human beings cannot apprehend Brahma through their senses. Men's sense information, it is claimed, is entirely inadequate. It is human and therefore limited; it is imperfect and Brahma is perfect. That which is known by definition cannot be the Brahma who is unknowable. Brahma's unknowability makes him more of an assertion or an assumption rather than a deity with whom the worshiper may have intimate and personal relations.

Yet Brahma sometimes is considered in personal terms. The form for designating him then may be changed; for example, in this context he may be referred to as Brahman. This connotation suggests that the one great god who is the creator of the world is knowable, that he has a personalized existence, and that worship is not foreign to his nature. Hindu mythology tends to strengthen this notion of Brahman. For instance, Brahman has a number of wives. One of them, Sarasvati, is said to have been born of Brahman. Like the Minerva of Roman religion, she is the goddess of science, speech, and music. The originator of Sanskrit script, she is pictured as elegant in form, white in color, without limbs that are unnecessary, yet riding about with a stringed instrument with which she makes music. In addition, Brahman in Hindu mythology has sons and daughters who perform various functions for him. Brahman himself is depicted in Hindu legends as having four bearded faces and four arms. In each arm he holds a scepter, a drinking bowl, a bow, and a Veda. He is said to ride a milk-white swan or goose about the highest *loka*. Obviously such characterizations of Brahman, including his family, are a far cry from the one, impersonal deity who stands beyond all known things, having finished his creation, now bearing essentially no vital relationship with the ongoing life of men.

Vishnu, the second major deity of the Hindu *trimurti,* was known in Vedic times, although it is clear that he was not a major god. In the Rig Veda he works together with Indra, then a more important deity, in Indra's efforts to subdue evil. Quite possibly Vishnu originated in Dravidian times. In the earlier times he was associated with good fortune and there are stories of that time which indicate that some of the other gods were jealous of his luck and sought to bring him harm. Later, however, Vishnu was associated with *dharma* (right action). He is the one deity who is thoroughly lawful, who believes in acting rightly, and who looks for no reward for so doing. Thus he is admired as an ideal of the devout Hindu. He is indeed a good god. Also, Vishnu is the protector and the sustainer of all good things. He takes an interest in maintaining righteousness by siding in all struggles that the good has with the bad. It is through his agency that the degree of goodness that exists is sustained. He prevents evil from taking over. In Hinduism he is the savior-god, the one who redeems mankind from its sins.

The worship of Brahma is not sustained by means of a cult. But Vishnu is the central god-figure of the cult of Vaishnava, which is one of the two major cults or sects of Hinduism. Although Vaishnavism is said by some to have originated in very early times, it more properly may be dated to medieval times. At this later period, Vishnu, following a long and varied development as a combination of prior gods and divine attributes, became the chief object of Vaishnavite worship. The sect lays considerable emphasis upon *bhakti* (devotion) to a personal deity. Vishnu is that god.

As the redeemer-god, Vishnu is not like the aloof Brahma. Vishnu is thoroughly knowable. He is an active deity who shares in human woes and aspirations. Although he is transcendent, he also has revealed himself directly and personally to human beings. He is known through his *avataras* (descents) from heaven to earth. These *avataras* are incarnations of Vishnu, but the use of this concept needs to be distinguished from its usage in other religions. In the case of Vishnu, for example, there have been ten principal incarnations and many more of lesser importance. Vishnu, in the ten main incarnations, has always appeared to save men from some evil. In one incarnation he became a boar in order to fight the demon Hiranyaksha. In another he took the form of a fish to save Vaivasvata, a semidivine king, from the deluge. Gautama, the founder of Buddhism, constitutes another of the *avataras*. Vishnu took the form of Buddha and founded a false faith so that the demons and perhaps men who are attracted to that religion will lose faith in the Vedas, break their caste obligations, deny the true gods of Hinduism, and so be led into damnation.

Vishnu's two chief incarnations, however, involve Rama and Krishna. These two *avataras* are held by the Vaishnavites to be the most significant manifestations of Vishnu in human form. A subsect within Vaishnavism is known as the Ramaites, and in it Rama is worshiped exclusively. Images of Rama are found throughout India and he is pictured in the company of his wife,

Sita; a devoted brother, Lakshmana; and an intensely loyal ser-
vant, Hanuman, a monkey-god who also is worshiped. Rama is
celebrated for many triumphs on the earth, but he is chiefly
revered for his slaying of Ravana, a powerful demon-king. Rama's
struggle with Ravana was long, involved, and tortuous. In shooting
his arrows at Ravana, for example, Rama found that for every
head of the demon-king that he hit, nine more heads sprang up.
Finally, with the help of Brahma, he used a new and divine
weapon. Throwing it, he split the heart of Ravana, who fell dead.
The conquering hero, after putting a good king on the throne,
returned to the first *loka*. The whole tale of this seventh incarnation is so complicated yet appealing that it forms the basis for
one of the great epics in Indian literature, the Ramayana, a *smriti*
scripture. Hindus love to recount the activities of Rama as they
are found in the Ramayana, taking courage for themselves and
for their children that Rama, the protector, is available to aid them
in their own struggles.

The eighth incarnation of Vishnu, that of Krishna, is thought
by many Hindus as being the most important. Krishna's story is
told mainly in the Mahabharata, perhaps the longest epic in the
world, and in the Bhagvata Purana. The Bhagavad Gita, which
is a section of the Mahabharata, is universally known and prized. It
tells of the exploits of Krishna as the heroic charioteer of Arjuna,
who engages in battle and conquers a host of enemies, sometimes through tricks. The Gita consists of a dialogue between Arjuna and Krishna, although the main body of the document consists
of Krishna's ideas on a variety of subjects and is taken by Vaishnavites as being the very words of deity. Krishna's exposition
stresses a pantheism which is close to that of the Upanishads. Only
the *atman*, or individual soul, and the Brahma truly exist. All else
is *maya* (illusion). The chief duty of man is duty itself. The person
should devote himself to *dharma* (right actions). In so doing, the
person should not be motivated by reward, but should be honorable
with no thought of recompense. The *dharma* in the context of
Krishna's teachings appears to consist of maintaining one's caste

obligations. Thus, when Arjuna draws back from undertaking a battle in which obviously many will be killed, Krishna responds by urging Arjuna to do his duty. The duty of *kshattriyas* (warriors) is to fight one's foes. Apparently Krishna is teaching that there is no morality which supersedes that of caste obligation. The Bhagavad Gita, then, gives sanction to fighting and killing. On the other hand, Krishna teaches that moderation is a key virtue. The holy person is one who is temperate, who leads an ascetic life, and who counts contemplation as a prime aim of life. Krishna also offers himself as the savior-god. He calls upon all men to worship him and states that salvation is available to all, including women and members of the lowest caste. He does not demand that worshipers follow any particular form and avers that he will bring satisfaction no matter how men worship him. This appeal of Krishna is the basis for the *bhakti*, or devotional aspect, of the Vaishnavite cult.

The tenth of Vishnu's *avataras* has not yet taken place, but will occur at the end of the present *kali-yurga* (age). Then he will come again, riding on a white horse.

Siva is the third major Hindu deity in the *trimurti*. While Brahma is the creator-god, and Vishnu is the protector-god, Siva is the destroyer-god. Siva represents those forces within the universe that encourage its disintegration. He is always tearing down. He is a god who instills fear in part, but he also is to be admired for his abilities and for his obvious power. He is terrifying and needs to be placated. Regularly in Hindu thought he is related to both death and time. Death is the final human evil, it would seem, and Siva is its responsible agent. Time also limits men in their hopes and their successes. Siva is the god of time. He is quite like the Dionysus of Greek legend.

But Siva has another side to him. He also is creative. His ambivalency is reflected in the idea that often destruction must necessarily precede construction, that what exists must be eliminated before something better or different can be made. The householder with a wooden porch that is aged and rotted must consider knocking it down before he will be able to replace it with a solid and perhaps more attractive edifice. So Siva is the destroyer-god who also accounts for much of what exists that is positive.

Siva, like the other gods, has a history. He is not known as such in the Rig Veda; there the word simply means "auspicious." Yet the worship of a god with Siva's attributes is known to be very ancient. He may have been brought into India by the Maga or some other tribe. Siva means "the red one." Another early name for him is Sambhu, which in the Tamil language also means "red" and connotes the reddish metal, copper. Rudra, another quite ancient god, also means "red one," and quite possibly there is a synthesis of the two early deities into the Siva who is well known and well accepted in later Hinduism.

Representations of Siva show him to have one or five faces. His four arms variantly hold various objects: fire, a small drum, the *mudras* (dance positions) of *abhaya* (protection) and *kriya* (action), a horn, a trident. Around him glows an arch of flames. Sometimes he is pictured with a third eye in the middle of his forehead, said to be the center of his destructive powers. It is with this eye, for example, that he burned Kama, the god of love, who tempted Siva's wife, Parvati, while Siva was doing penance. Married, he has two children: Ganesa and Karttikeya.

Siva is associated with destruction and creativity. In his destructive context he is a harsh, flesh-eating deity who delights in bloody sacrifices. These blood sacrifices involve animals, although at times in the past human beings also were subjects. He also is pleased to have as his friends all those spirits, ghosts, ghouls, and other esoteric beings who haunt cemeteries, drink the blood of dead persons, and scare human beings with their dire activities. One story, for example, in Hindu mythology tells about a demonic creature, Kirtimukha, who was created by Siva for the purpose of fighting Rahu. Rahu is a terrible, four-armed *danava* (titan) who was dragon-tailed. Rahu constantly gave both Vishnu and Siva trouble. His exploits are told in the Ramayana. Kirtimukha was so fierce in face that Radhu begged to be spared without a

battle. Since the titan had been created to eat Radhu, he demand-
ed a meal of Siva. Siva instructed Kirtimukha to eat his own feet,
which the titan did, following this by eating the rest of his body
until only his head remained. The titan's head was saved and representations of it are used as a talisman among the faithful who worship Siva. The story illustrates the ferocity of Siva.

Siva, by contrast, also is associated with love. The *linga* (phallus) is a favorite symbol of his followers and is widely used as an
object of veneration. Combined with the *linga* is the *yoni* (female
sexual organ), sometimes referred to as the womb. Apparently
linga worship is very ancient within Hinduism. The Aryans were
surprised by such worship as they found it among the Dravidians.
The Rig Veda indicates that it was a point of significant difference
between the two peoples. But gradually the acceptance of *linga*
worship among the combined peoples established it as a feature of
Hinduism. Siva's worship historically and presently is the most
prominent expression of this development. Siva's consort, Sakti,
also figures in this kind of worship. Despite its past, *linga* worship
today is not considered by many Hindus to be particularly erotic
for human beings, but constitutes a formal symbolism of the
creative aspects of Siva.

The worship of Siva, like that of Vishnu, is supported by a cult or
sect. This is one of the strong bases it has for being a leading force
in Hinduism. The religion centered in Siva is known as Saivism
and the followers as Saivites. While the Saivites hold much in
common with the Vaishnavites, they are distinctive in certain
matters. One of these distinctions is the stress placed among the
Saivites on asceticism. Despite the history of *linga* worship, the
Saivites also find in Siva their model for withdrawal from worldly
activities and their concentration upon contemplation as a religious requirement. The Lingayats, for example, a sect within
Saivism, are austere worshipers of Siva. They do not drink alcoholic beverages, use tobacco, or take drugs. The most devoted
among them are celibate and most of them are connected with a
monastery.

Of special interest and importance for an understanding of Saivism is the worship of Sakti, Siva's consort. Sakti, the mother goddess, has become an important deity in her own right and is widely worshiped in India. Actually, the term *sakti* (energy) is applied to the wives of many of the gods. For some of the gods, such as Indra, Rudra, and Varuna, their wives are relatively dormant. They are recognized as wives and comprise the duality of the single deity. At other times, however, the gods' consorts are considered to be the active principle within creation, the male counterpart being more remote and static. In such cases the female deity may be viewed as the equal of her male counterpart; in other cases, such as Radha, Sita, and Durga, the wife is deemed to be even more important.

Sakti, the wife of Siva, is given special prominence among the *sakti* worshipers. In fact, the mother goddess, Sakti, often is thought to be of greater significance than Siva himself. She is considered to be the more complete one, that divine force which precedes all others, and the basis for the creative activities even of Brahma, the creator-god. A number of cults have sprung up in Hinduism, commonly called the Sakta cults, which give the principal honor to Sakti. These cults are supported by a large literature, including the Tantras. Tantrism, a form of Hinduism which is based upon the Tantras, like Sakta worship, is considered a left-handed development in religion. This means that such religion seeks to honor everything that the regular religionist thinks is not worthy of honor. That which the world holds in low esteem, Tantrism claims, actually should be revered and practiced. So the worship of Sakti fits this description and the assumption gives support to the worship of the female over the male principle.

Ritualism in Hinduism is classified into two types: (1) Vedic ritualism based, of course, upon the teachings of the Vedas as they have been developed and reinforced in the Brahmanas and elsewhere; (2) the *agamic*, which is based on the Agamas as these have been developed by various sects. Probably chief among the *agamic* forms are those offered in Tantrism. Although Tantrism is not in itself a cult, it has given rise to a number of cults which, each in its own way, follow the general teachings. Tantrism, moreover, is not in itself an exclusive philosophy, although it offers in some of its parts philosophical teachings that are profound. Tantrism is essentially a set of beliefs and practices that pervade many aspects of the thought and practice of a large number of Hindus. Tantrism also influenced Buddhism and a Buddhist Tantrism exists which is essentially foreign to traditional Buddhism.

The teachings of Tantrism are found in the Tantras. In the main these were composed in Hinduism's medieval period. Although its advocates believe the Tantras to be superior to the Vedas, the largest part of them is still untranslated. Some of the Tantras are considered so base that Hindus are not anxious that they be translated, and undoubtedly some of them have been destroyed by orthodox Hindus and by Muslims who were offended by them. They chiefly take the form of dialogues between Siva and his wife, Sakti, and they consist of reflections upon the creation and dissolution of the universe, proper modes for worshiping the gods, certain spiritual exercises, the ways in which magical powers may be used to one's advantage, various rituals, and to a minor degree some guides to meditation.

As suggested, occultism is important in Tantrism. Tantrism teaches how a person can use various objects, such as flowers, bells, incense, and candles, in sorcery. It uses *mantras* (magical spells), *mandalas* (magical diagrams), special postures and breathing practices, cultic nudity, exercises involving cadavers, graveyards' ordure, and other matters and activities in order to gain control over the darker forces in life.

Sexuality also is a key element in Tantrism, but sexuality, like the other features of Tantrism, is understood in what Hindus call a left-handed way. This way reverses the commonly held view of good and bad. That which is regularly considered to be bad in ordinary society is viewed as good in Tantrism. So sexuality is utilized in a left-handed way. This means that followers are released from the usual restraints and take delight and religious merit in various perversions, including incest. The follower, more-over, also believes that after practicing human perversions he ascends religiously by engaging in practices with the demons and other beings of the nether-world. Finally, if he reaches the second plateau, he seeks to have sexual relation even with the gods and goddesses. Thus sexuality, a central feature of Tantrism, is held to possess both natural and supernatural power and is an in-dispensable factor in religious expression.

Manifestations

The various Hindu deities also are characterized by various kinds of manifestations. The *avataras* (descents) of some of the gods already have been mentioned. These comprise highly signifi-cant and special manifestations. The gods also are *vibhava* (re-splendent). They appear to select persons in radiant form. Such a theophany differs from the *avatara* in that it suggests a vision available to the faithful rather than an actual incarnation. Such *vibhava* of Siva and Sakti are held to be possible and are said to take place among the most faithful of the Saivites. The Vaishna-vites, one the other hand, are inclined to speak of another type of manifestation, especially of Vishnu, which is called *vyuha*, or an extension of the deity. These extensions commonly take the nature of the five forms of existence: supreme being, absolute knowledge, individual soul, mind, and self-consciousness. In wide usage also in Hinduism is the notion of *vahana* (vehicle). The *vahana* usually is a bird or an animal who is associated with the particular god. In early Hinduism *vahanas* are not found, but by the time of the Puranas they were attached to almost all of the major deities. These creatures serve the deity and to some extent reflect the deity. Examples of the gods and their *vahanas* are: Agni, the ram; Brah-ma, the swan; Durga, the lion or the tiger; Kama, the parrot; Lakshmi, the owl; Siva, a white bull; Varuna, a sea-monster; Vishnu, the eagle and the serpent; and Yama, the buffalo.

Hinduism in its long and complicated history has sought to express man's respect for the divine. Despite some *nastika* tendencies, it is a believing religion. It calls upon men to believe in the divine. It perceives the divine to be all-encompassing in human affairs. Gods are seen within the daily life in concrete and manifold ways. They are also operative in forming and maintaining the conditions for human society. Their paths can be discerned throughout the universe. Hinduism provides enough variety in concepts of the divine to satisfy the longings and beliefs of everyone. It traditionally does not press for literal and exclusive definitions of the divine, but is content to let plurality itself be a virtue. A thread of monism and theism extends from very ancient times through this pluralism, but all human conceptions are viewed with some suspicion and doubt, for the Hindu believes that men, despite their heroic endeavors to apprehend the divine through their intellectual efforts, are severely limited and imperfect. So the divine may better be known through allegorical representations, the universe being not scientific but, rather, mythopoetic in nature. Existence is not so much fact as it is drama. The forces of subjectivity are much to be prized over those of objectivity. Believing in the divine is more important than any man-made conception of the divine.

SIX

Popular Religion

All historic religions that have survived through many centuries and have appealed to large numbers of peoples have taken many forms and possess many attributes. In fact, it may at times seem difficult if not impossible to describe them as particular religions at all. Their very diversity in their organized development, including major and minor branches, suggests that they are more divided than united. The variety of their theological doctrines may indicate that they have little fundamental conviction which binds all followers. The diverse ways in which the intellectually inclined have related themselves to philosophic issues may provide no assurance to those who seek rational unity. The many practices of worship also may appear to further dissolve any pretense that a religion can be satisfactorily defined and limited. In this mood, perhaps most tempting to scholars, a religion, like Hinduism, may seem to be too elusive to be caught in a definitional trap, too varied and vague to be encompassed by the classroom or the written page.

The great historic religions, however, are tremendously complex and they do manage to evade successful definition. The effort to describe and define is essentially an activity in delimitation, and such an activity usually seeks to narrow rather than broaden one's perspective. To some extent all such efforts tend to be self-defeating. They in part rest upon methods which say that something is this and not that, when in actuality it may be both and indeed more. So it is with religions and especially with Hinduism. From one perspective it may seem that Hinduism simply cannot be described and defined satisfactorily. Probably it cannot. Efforts to delimit it are regularly made and should be made. But the patient observer should also realize that Hinduism is too large and complex to be caught in any one net. Yet it must be said that Hinduism is a religion; it is a term which has a usage both by those who follow it and by those who stand outside it. It is a religion.

The popular expression of a historic religion constitutes one among several ways in which a religion is itself. Sectarian formulations, philosophic activities, cultic practices, social observances, the regulations that govern the individual's life—all are part of the totality of a religion. Viewed in special ways these aspects may seem to be separable, yet for full understanding they must be placed together in a coherent fashion. Hinduism's popular religion, then, is one expression of the totality of that religion. It is the Hinduism that is observed, especially in the many forms of worship. It is not the least or the most worthy form of Hinduism; it is simply one aspect of a very complex and fascinating religion. It is composed of such features as worship in general, festivals, pilgrimages, the temple, the home, ritual, and other matters.

In Hinduism the highest form of worship is said to be reserved for Brahma. Since Brahma is *nirguna* (without attributes), this kind of worship has few social expressions. He who is nameless does not call for his naming in rituals, sacrifices, and other elements of worship. Brahma is a subject for individual meditation. One seeks to become one with him, but this oneness is not achievable through elaborate ceremony. The second form of worship recognizes Brahma as Brahman, or a deity with *saguna* (attributes). Deities other than Brahma also possess *saguna* and are, therefore, worshipable through the employment of fairly concrete means. About such gods as Vishnu and Siva, for example, well-developed sects have grown up, offering the believer a rich collection of worship possibilities. The third, and by far most popular form of worship, involves a *pratika* or symbol of a god as a practical center for worship. Commonly the *pratika* may be almost any natural object, but often it is an idol. In actuality these three forms of worship are not exclusive. A Hindu may recognize and practice all three. For those, however, who are not inclined to the requirements of the first two, the third appears to be the most accepted and useful.

Idols

The worship of idols has existed in all periods in Hinduism's history. The Aryans, however, seem not to have been idolaters at first. Certainly the Vedas have no developed doctrine of idol worship and in fact they seem to disparage those who engage in the practice. Probably, then, idol worship was known by the indigenous peoples prior to the invasion of the Aryans. The Magas and the Vratyas peoples, for example, are known to have practiced *linga* worship. Possibly such practice was based upon very ancient fertility cults which included phallus-shaped objects, usually of stone, as elements of their worship. The Aryans originally held such worshipers in contempt, and the Rig Veda contains injunctions against them. Yet by the time of the epics the Aryans seem to have relented and indeed to have taken over the practice of *linga* worship from those whom they much earlier had despised.

At any rate, the worship of idols did become a fixture of Aryan as well as other worship in India. By the time of the Mahabharata, for example, idol worship was taken for granted and, in the Ramayana, Rama himself is portrayed as giving an idol of himself as a chief present to a temple. Such reform movements as Jainism and Buddhism in their earliest phases rejected idol worship and were in this regard reactions against the easy and widespread acceptance of idols in Hinduism. But they in turn developed their own systems of idols and in the end gave even added impetus to the further growth of idol worship within Hinduism.

Idolatry has been criticized in almost every generation in Hinduism. The reformers of the modern period, with some exceptions, have spoken sharply against the practice. They have ridiculed it as absolutely worthless and indeed an impediment to true, or the higher forms of, worship. Some have tolerated idol worship as a force running too deep in Indian life to be easily eradicated. Others have denied the efficacy of idolatry, but have felt that it is helpful to the religiously ignorant, a necessary feature of popular religion. Many orthodox Hindus, however, believe that the idol is not merely a material object, shaped by human hands, but is in reality the resident location of a god. They say that an idol is not merely one device among others of symbolizing a god, but the god himself. While others seek ways by which to explain away the actual worship of idols, the orthodox ask for no such rationalizations. They indeed worship idols as the gods themselves.

The proper creation of an idol is no easy task. The person making it usually consults with the astrologers, who aid him in determining the best time and circumstances. The sculptor also undergoes certain rites by which he is purified and made ready. His choice of material is important. Some idols, for example, are made of clay for special occasions, for use during festivals, and then are crushed and dropped into a river. The material used for a more permanent deity must be considered in terms of the god and his particular attributes. Stones and metals have different potentialities. The precise form of the idol also has significance; the number of arms and legs are carefully counted as well as the objects that the hands may grasp. Idols made of wood are taken from appropriate trees that are cut at an auspicious time, and dried and fashioned in prescribed ways. Finally the placement of the idol, whether at home or in a temple, requires ceremonies regarding the site, the manner of emplacement, and the actual giving of "life" to the idol. In these and other ways the production of idols permits no caprice, but is bound by a complex set of ritualistic requirements.

In addition to idols, Hinduism also shows an unusual concern with animals. Traditionally it has sought to classify the creatures of land, air, and sea, and has held all natural life, including the fauna, in high regard. Among all the creatures, however, the cow has been held in the highest regard and cow worship is widely practiced within India and is well known outside India as a feature of Hinduism. A brief description of cow worship will illustrate another aspect of popular religion. Again, as in the worship of idols, cow worship is very ancient in India. Like the worship of the cow goddess, Hathor, in ancient Egypt, cow worship in early India was associated with the worship of the mother-goddess. Worship of the bull also was known in pre-Vedic times, but by the time of the Vedas the cow came into prominence, possibly as a result of the facts that the cow gave both life-nourishing milk and more bulls which could be used in the work of the fields. Thus the Rig Veda speaks of the cow as *aghnya* (nonkillable), although the slaying of bulls was practiced both for human eating and for sacrificial purposes. Apparently there was no taboo on meat-eating in Vedic times. Later, however, especially when the brahmins took a hand in codifying Hinduism, cow slaughter was deemed a sin and cow worship a key virtue. By the time of the Puranas the cow was claimed to have been created on the same day as Brahman, and his several parts were thought to be the residencies of particular gods. During the Gupta dynasty (*ca.* A.D. 320-467) the killing of cows became a capital offense, and it is even recorded that one king had his own son killed when the boy accidentally killed a cow. Some Hindus still wish for a national law against cow-killing, and on occasion there are communal riots in India when a Muslim, who is bound by no such injunction, kills a cow. Even Gandhi, for example, felt strongly bound by cow worship and held the cow to be in some respects more worthy than a human mother.

Not only is the cow held in high esteem and worshiped widely in India, but its products also are considered sacred by many. Thus some Hindus say that whatever comes out of a cow also is worthy of deep respect. The five products of the cow that are held in such reverence are milk, *ghee* (clarified butter), curds, cow dung, and cow urine.

Cow urine is used in ceremonial bathing and in connection with pregnant women. Cow dung is mixed with dirt and used in village huts to purify them. In popular Hinduism, then, cow worship has a notable place.

In fact, all things, both animate and inanimate, are viewed in Hinduism as possessing *prabhava* (splendor). This occultly derived attribute is conceived as a kind of luminosity or potency which on occasion breaks forth. Persons are said to possess it. So a priest or even those who participate in worship have this quality and its presence is shared. The objects of worship and aids to worship have this psychic aura. If such an object or aid is broken or contaminated, its condition must be propitiated so that it may be restored with its proper *prabhava*. Even in secular life, the bricklayer, for example, whose brick inadvertently breaks in two, seeks to restore the *prabhava* by a rite. It is the *prabhava* which is the potency in medicines, enabling them to do their curative work. The *yajamana* (sacrificer) is especially careful to maintain his splendor both before and during his ceremonies. If he must urinate during a ceremony, for example, he must dig a special hole in the ground with a horn and urinate in that, the rest of the earth being for that time profane. Similarly the *yajamana* believes that water will wash away his *prabhava* and so he avoids washing or being caught in the rain. Following his ceremony he speaks the *mantras* so that his splendor may properly be extinguished. Objects utilized in the ceremony then are washed in order to return them to their preceremonial status. The *prabhava*, moreover, is thought to be both good and bad. Some ceremonial objects, such as the post and spit used in sacrifices, must be purified following their use so that harm will not result. Objects having *prabhava* also are used on occasion to practice divination, and some *yajamanas* are able to read into the features of such objects various signs that foretell the future. Popular Hinduism thus overcasts all things with *prabhava*, a special splendor with religious connotations.

Festivals

Hindus seize upon many occasions to celebrate and their calendar is heavily marked by religious holidays. These holidays are festive occasions in which popular religion takes one of its principal forms. The Hindus have a highly developed sense of time, not only for the ages of man and the *kalpa* of the universe, but for particular days and events. Certain days, for example, when a full moon falls on a particular day of the week, are special days. Deeds of service to others done on that day are particularly meritorious. Similarly, rituals performed on auspicious days are more than usually potent. Other kinds of special days or seasons are related to events in nature, such as the several seasons. Thanksgiving for the harvest and, in the spring, festivals to ensure fertility are in order. Other natural objects also merit festivals: snakes, rivers, cows, buffalos, one's guru, stones, monkeys, thread, ancestors, smallpox, plants, various spirits, hills, and chariots. Of course, festivals are held to honor the gods. Practically all the major gods have their festivals, while quite a number of festivals are also devoted to the lesser gods. Sometimes the festivals celebrate a mythological event in which the deity is supposed to have participated. So the Gita Jayanti is a festival which is observed during November-December to celebrate the occasion when Krishna delivered the Bhagavad Gita to Arjuna.

Several of the festivals may be identified briefly to illustrate the very much larger number. The Divali, sometimes called Dipavali in Sanskrit, is one of the more important Hindu festivals. In a minimal sense this festival is like Christmas in that it occurs in the wintertime and is marked by the use of lights. On the night of the new moon in October-November worship, it is celebrated by filling small earthen bowls with oil and placing them lit in rows both inside and outside homes and temples. Actually Divali lasts for five days. Also, it really consists of a number of festivals or differing parts of the one festival. On the first day, the goddesses Lakshmi and Parvati, or Sakti, are honored, and the members of the trading castes worship Lakshmi, the goddess of wealth, by various ceremonies involving coins, such as coloring coins and placing them before the goddess's image. Gambling is the main theme of the second day. Men and women use dice on this day to commemorate the reconciliation of Siva and Sakti. Women also create colorful and complicated geometric designs in and out of their homes. On the third day, the victory of Vishnu over the demon king Bali (or Naraka) is celebrated. This day has regional variants. In Bengal, Kali, the black goddess is worshiped. In some places in south India Bali is worshiped. Usually though in the evening, following a day of fasting, Lakshmi is worshiped. The fourth day is marked by the bowls of light in rows at dusk. The trading caste marks its new year on this day. The fifth and final day is devoted to Yama, the god of the departed spirits. On this day every man is obligated to dine in the house of a female relative, such as a sister or cousin; he also gives her presents on this day. The *kayastha* (clerical caste) acknowledges Chitragupta, the clerk of Yama, according to Hindu mythology. So Divali closes.

Holi is another major Hindu festival. Because it involves the lighting of bonfires it also is referred to as Hutasani, or fire-consuming. It takes place about ten days before the full moon in February-March, although in practice only the last three or four days are observed. The bonfires are thought to burn out all evil. Also, a maypole is used and people parade about it, as they do on the streets generally, blowing horns, pounding on drums or pots and pans, shouting and making noise. During Holi, moreover, *dolayatra* (swinging rites) are featured. Platforms with swings are built and arranged with flowers. Images of certain deities are then placed in the swings, which are then swung to the accompaniment of singing and dancing Hindus. Sometimes a woman is placed in the swing to indicate her intimate surrender to Krishna. The swing rites are especially popular and the concept of swinging is widely believed in Hinduism to have sexual connotations and to represent a means of transcending the earthly and entering, perhaps through the consequence of dizziness, a state which is not entirely human. Paradise, for example, is characterized as a place where the gods and goddesses deport themselves in swings. Swinging rites are employed at other times than Holi. During Holi, furthermore, a distinctive practice is the use of colored powders and liquids that the celebrant puts on himself and also sprinkles freely on others who are engaged in worshiping.

The Naga-panchami festival, celebrated on one day in July-August, is devoted chiefly to the snake. Mythologically the day is said to celebrate the victory of Krishna over the serpent Kaliya. On this day, which begins with a fast, bathing in the mass occurs in rivers and images of snakes also are bathed. The faithful also refrain from plowing their fields so that they will not inadvertently kill a snake. Further, they locate holes in the ground where snakes are known to live and there place various objects that are thought to benefit the creatures: water and milk to drink, a comb and a mirror for preening, cooked food or just flour for eating. The snake, mythological and real, is the center of the Naga-panchami festival, one of a very large number of festivals that are prominent features of popular Hinduism.

Pilgrimages

Going on religious pilgrimages is another feature of Hindu popular religion. It is very widely practiced and may be classified as a form of worship. *Yatra* ("going") is based upon a number of factors. Obviously it is appealing to the desire of people to travel. By traveling to holy sites Hindus are able to see new parts of their land, to meet other followers of the faith, and to enrich their own store of knowledge. But *yatra* also is significant because of religious reasons. The faithful person is able to demonstrate his respect for a deity. He is able to secure certain personal merits for this life and the next. If he is a member of a sect, he is able to strengthen his feelings of solidarity with those who believe as he does. The pilgrim, moreover, is participating in the Hindu sense of *prabhava* (splendor) which surrounds and invades the whole of life, animate and inanimate. India is a holy land in many respects, and it contains thousands of places that shine with this splendor for the devout.

Sometimes religious festivals and pilgrimages are combined activities. The Kumbha-mela, for example, is an apt example. It is a festival which is held every three years at four places: Allahabad at the junction of the Ganges and the Jumna, Hardwar on the Ganges, Ujjain on the Kshipra, and Nasik on the Godavari. These four spots are sacred because in Indian mythology some demons either stopped at these places or dropped sacred nectar there, hallowing the sites. Millions of Hindus assemble at the sites and engage in huge festivals. Earlier Kumbha-melas were occasions for various criminal activities, including rape, murder, and rioting. They still draw large numbers of persons who prey on the faithful. But they also appeal to the multitudes who bathe in the sacred waters and are cleansed of their sins. Some bring pots of seeds that they dip into the river and later, in conjunction with other seeds, plant with the expectation of getting good crops. Women who are barren believe that they can be made fertile through rites performed at the Kumbha-mela. Intellectually inclined Hindus find in the *melas* a ready forum for discussion and debate; sectarians have a means of meeting other sectarians.

An almost endless number of holy places exist to which the loyal Hindu may make his pilgrimage. *Pithas* (footrests) exist which are said to be the places where the limbs of the mother-goddess fell when her body was severed by Vishnu's wheel. Various places are connected with water. A *tirtha* (a ford on a river) is regularly an object of pilgrimage. Sacred lakes throughout India serve this purpose. *Asramas* (study places for holy men) are also gathering places for pilgrims who seek increased knowledge.

The Ganges is an especially sacred river and is believed to have had divine origins. In the beginning the Ganges flowed only in the first *loka*; its source was Vishnu's toe. There it made the celestial region fertile. But permission was secured to have the Ganges come to the earth. Its torrential flow was so great that the safety of the earth was threatened until Siva permitted it to flow through his locks, slowing it up and forming the seven sacred rivers of India. The seven are: Ganges, Jumna, Sarasvati, Godavari, Narmada, Indus, and Kaveri, although the last two vary with the Tapti and the Kistna. All rivers, but particularly these seven, are considered divine; they also are considered to be female. Associated with fertility, the rivers are thought to have a variety of other powers, including the ability to wash away sins. A bath in the Ganges is particularly potent. The bones and ashes of the deceased are often placed in the Ganges in the belief that the dead person will inherit everlasting bliss. A diseased person who bathes in the Ganges, especially using a disciplined posture, such as standing on one leg, may be healed. A person who by his own decision drowns in the river also goes to paradise. Even to drink the water, noted for its contamination, helps the drinker gain benefits in the after life as well as this life. All in all, the Ganges is held to be very powerful in its benefits to the believer and is the object of pilgrimage for a great many.

Hindus consider certain cities also to be sacred places and make pilgrimages to them. In earlier times three cities were deemed to be special: Prayaga, Kasi or Banaras, and Gaya. In more recent times seven are commonly mentioned; they are, in addition to the prior three: Ayodhya, Mathura, Hardwar, and Dvaraka. Banaras, for example, is located on the Ganges. The city, now known as Varanasi, is rich in mythological references, for it was here that Brahman offered ten horses in sacrifice, Siva practiced austerities, and other superhuman events took place. The city is a congeries of religious sites with perhaps more than a thousand temples and several hundreds of thousands of idols. Saivites consider it their central place of worship and have built a temple about a *linga* image, one of such *linga* centers for the cult in India which are objects of pilgrimage. There is a most sacred area within the city which is bounded by a thirty-six-mile roadway. Many elderly Hindus are brought to this area to spend their final days, because it is affirmed that anyone, despite caste, past life, or any other qualification, who dies in the sacred area will inherit paradise. Pilgrims to Banaras secure religious merit by walking around the sacred jurisdiction; usually this takes six days. The river front in Banaras is especially replete with temples and *ghats* (bathing places). Banaras is the most holy of the seven holy cities of Hinduism.

The pilgrim takes part in a number of activities once he has reached his destination. He will usually take a ritual bath in purifying water. He will worship the god who is related to the place. He also will give presents to the brahmins who attend the shrine. Sometimes he hires a hierophant to assist him with the successful completion of all of his obligations. In addition, the rite of *pradakshina* (circumambulation) is held in high regard. With the object or shrine to his right, the worshiper walks about it— thus assuring merit. Circumambulation in general is valued by Hindus and reflects the importance which is ascribed to the wheel in Indian life. Every part of the wheel is thought to have symbolic significance. The turning of the wheel to the right is suggestive of rightness and is used, for example, by the pious in turning cylinders of sacred writings. In a Hindu marriage ceremony the groom leads the bride three times around the altar in the "right" way. In death ceremonies, on the other hand, mourners walk about the corpse in the left way. So at sacred places that are the objects of pilgrimage, circumambulation is also practiced around a temple, an altar, a holy book or person. The six-day walk at Banaras is a *pradakshina* appropriately marked with a number of stations. The river Ganges may be circumambulated according to a plan which takes the worshiper six years to accomplish.

Every able Hindu takes part in a pilgrimage of some sort. He may go far or near, but he believes that he is expressing a religious requirement that will bring him various benefits. While on his way he will usually stop at intermediate pilgrimage places to render homage even though these may not be of his own sect or even of his own religion. *Yatra* is a widespread, deeply felt aspect of popular Hinduism.

Temples

The Hindu, however, does not need to go far from home in order to worship. The home itself is a major center of religious expression and as such will be discussed in Chapter 9 in some detail. But the Hindu also holds the temple to be an important center of his worship. Many thousands of temples exist in India, varying in almost every respect. Visually they form a constant reminder of the pervasiveness of Hinduism. They are so plentiful that almost every believer has an opportunity physically to be related to a temple. They provide the person also with a dramatic portrayal on a daily basis of the great drama of life itself.

The temples vary greatly in size and complexity. In a small village the temple may be very small indeed. It may appear to be little more than a wayside shrine. Its statuary by many artistic standards would be judged as crude. Simplicity and lack of cost would be common. Yet these temples have significant meaning for the villager, for to him this temple is the locus of his worship. On the other hand, Hindu temples in some instances are marked by extreme size and beauty. The temple at Puri is an example at the opposite extreme from that of the village shrine. Jagannatha (warlord) is the deity who is worshiped at Puri. He is regionally worshiped as a form of Krishna. The temple is very large and complex and actually is not one but many temples. The temple grounds are surrounded with a stone wall that is twenty feet high. The grounds measure more than six hundred feet on each side. Within this enclosure are several temples, some of which are dedicated to Vishnu, Krishna, Siva, and other gods. The chief temple is dedicated to Jagannatha and to the brother and sister of Krishna, Balabhadra and Subhadra. The tower of Jagannatha's temple measures about two hundred feet in height. The Puri temple is managed by about six thousand persons. They are divided into thirty-six orders and ninety-seven classes, and include guides, warders, attendants, and priests. Some of these awaken the deities, dress them and give them food, and help them retire for the night. Divers bands of dancing girls also perform throughout the day for the entertainment of the gods. Not everyone in Puri makes a living from the temple, but it is said that as many as twenty thousand persons are related to the functioning of the temple.

This temple illustrates not only the size and complexity of some Hindu temples; it also shows how a temple may be the center of festivals of note and for pilgrimages. Thousands of pilgrims gather twice a year at Puri's temple to engage in two festivals. One is devoted to the annual bathing of the temple idols. The other is perhaps more picturesque and takes six days for its completion. During this festival a huge *ratha* (wooden chariot), finely ornamented, is pulled through the streets by more than four thousand assigned men. The image of Jagannatha predominates the chariot, which has sixteen wheels each seven feet in diameter. The chariot also is thirty-five feet square and forty-five feet high. This procession, held in an auspicious time in June-July, is truly impressive in its magnitude and even in its beauty. After each year's procession the chariot is broken up and the pieces are sold as relics. The chariot for the next year is then built. Every twelve or twenty-four years the idols used in the procession also are broken up and made afresh. In the past a few persons thrust themselves under the heavy wheels of the chariot and suffered death in the belief that by so doing they would go straight to paradise, but the British succeeded in stopping this practice.

Whether large or small, a temple is originally built to certain specifications carefully outlined in the religious literature. Hindus speak of the temple as *mandira,* or a place of gladdening. The temple is devoted not to the worshiper but to a god. The essential requirement, therefore, of every temple is that it have a *vimana* (shrine) which in turn has a *garbha-griha* (womb-house or little cell) in which the god in the form of an idol or some other representation is placed. This is the prime requirement and all other features of the temple are auxiliary to the housing of the deity to whom the temple is dedicated. In early times the *vimana* was all there was to a temple. Possibly then the temple was simply a hut, like the other huts, in composition that were used for homes and other purposes. Perhaps then as now the temples had sloping towers to distinguish them from other buildings. These towers, called *sikhara,* which means "summit," have been thought to represent the celestial realms that are associated with the transcendent aspects of the gods, places from whence they came and in which they feel at home.

The temple oftentimes has grown from its earliest form and most basic requirement. In some there is a second *garbha-griha,* which is provided for the god's consort. In others the temple is surrounded by a wall and the wall's entrance features a *gopura* (monumental gate), which is elaborately striking in its appearance. Many temples have hypostylic additions which are called *mandapa,* or pillared halls, in which the worshipers and others conduct their worship activities. In his approach to the *mandapa* the worshiper passes a *yupa* (sacrifical post) on his left. This post, derived from Vedic times, is where sacrifical animals were tied. Even today, however, in some parts of India such as Bengal, actual sacrifices are made and the post is used. In many temples today the *yupa* has become a *dhvaja* (flagstaff). It also may be a decorated column, the column having religious significance in itself in Hinduism.

In large temples room is provided for a variety of activities that are connected with worship. A room may be reserved for the storing of consecrated items used in worship, another for the sacred fire, yet another for the preparation of the sacrificial food. In the temple compound provision may be made for buildings devoted to the dancing girls of the temple, for schools, monasteries, and even hospitals. Thus the temple in its most complex form involves a multiplicity of functions with structures that reflect this diversity. Regional and other variations also regulate the nature of the Hindu temple.

Religious Leadership

The priesthood which serves the temple reflects the nature of the temple. Many of the smaller temples have no priest. Where size and other considerations require one, the *pujari* (temple priest) is regularly not given high status. Being looked down upon, he lives on whatever is voluntarily contributed to him in the form of alms. The larger temples, of course, have a correspondingly elaborate priesthood with one priest in charge. The chief priest may have a number of assistants. These will have their own duties: attending the temple fire, serving the sacrificial food, performing the daily sprinkling ceremony, and managing other aspects of the temple routine. Some assistants may be provided for teaching duties, so that those faithful who wish religious instruction may have it. Other priests perform their responsibilities in the homes of the devout.

The fact is that the priest is not the only religious leader who holds the respect of the faithful. Other kinds of religious specialists are found in Hinduism; the guru, for example. Hinduism assumes that the path to *moksha* (salvation) is not easy and that every believer is in need of a highly qualified mentor who will assist him in a disciplined manner to obtain his goal. Unlike the priest who is a specialist in ritual, the guru is basically a student-teacher. The guru is one who has devoted his life to study, especially the study of the sacred scriptures. He is essentially an intellectual who applies reasoning to religious questions. He also is a teacher, set aside by the community to instruct learners in the fundamentals of Hinduism.

The guru, also called an *acharya* or spiritual teacher, practices what he preaches. In this connotation the teacher is not one who is concerned with truth in an abstract way, but is himself a human exemplification of the truth. The *acharya* is one who demonstrates in his own life the combination of truth with action. The *acharya* is able to impart truth to his follower, but he also is able by example to put the learner on the correct path by which the *acharya* himself has succeeded in the spiritual quest.

Other specialists within Hinduism include the swami, the *sadhu,* the yogi, the *sannyasin,* the astrologer, the pandit, and others. The swami is usually a member of a religious order, a special group that has taken vows of poverty, chastity, and obedience to the order. In some cases the term is applied only to the senior members of the order or is restricted even to the chief swami. The *sadhu* is a holy man who expresses his virtue in ascetic practices. Commonly he is not a member of any order and does not come under the discipline of others. The yogi is anyone who is self-disciplined in his search for *moksha.* He usually practices those exercises that have developed in the Yoga system of philosophy or in such other aspects of popular Hinduism as Tantrism. The *sannyasin* is a person who has reached a prescribed stage of individual life in which withdrawal from the world, at least to a marked degree, and the undergoing of ascetic and other disciplines are his chosen lot. Usually he devotes a major part of his time to the taking of instruction from a guru. The astrologer reflects in his occupation the fact that Hinduism, especially in its popular aspects, depends heavily upon an understanding of propitious times and methods of acting. Popular Hinduism teaches that there is a proper time and place for everything, and the astrologer is set apart by the community to manage these concerns. The term *pandit* (scholar) also is used for those persons to whom one may bring specific questions about conduct that affects one's well-being in the future. Obviously the prescribed functions of these various specialists of religious leadership within Hinduism overlap to a greater or less degree. One person may enjoy more than one designation or status.

For example, a yogi may also be a guru, a *sannyasin,* or a swami. Other combinations also are possible.

Until the turn of the last century another form of religious specialist attached to the temple was the *devadasi* (the god's slave), the temple prostitute. The practice of temple prostitution is very old in Hinduism. One of the Puranas, for example, speaks of the purchase of young women for this purpose. In the seventh century A.D. a Chinese traveler, Hiuen-Tsang, was astonished at the large number of temple prostitutes at Multan. Also, it is said that in the tenth century A.D. King Rajaraja built a temple at Tanjore and included four hundred such women for it. Temple prostitution in Hinduism was considered a religious rather than a secular occupation. The *devadasi* was not looked down upon; rather, she was thought of as a member of a profession of some standing. She was envied by many women and her presence was sought at weddings and other events as a sign of the favor of the gods. Girls historically were recruited into this service in a number of ways. Sometimes a couple with no male heir would give a daughter to the temple with the understanding that the daughter for ritual and familial purposes would secure the status of a son, performing the especially important funeral rites and even inheriting property as would a son. Couples would also give a daughter to the temple in fulfillment of a promise made to a deity for some benefit that was received. If a couple's firstborn were a daughter, they might pledge her to the temple in the hope that the god of the temple would provide them later with a son. Unmarried daughters, moreover, have always been considered economic handicaps, by reason of the dowry system and otherwise, and some couples would give unwanted daughters to the temple as a means of getting rid of them. Through these and other ways, then, *devadasis* were secured.

Once installed in the temple, usually at the age of seven or eight, the initiate underwent certain rites by which she was married to the god, was trained in dancing or other temple requirements, was deflowered by the chief priest or a stone *linga,* and was made available to worshipers. The income of the *devadasis* was turned over to the temple priests. As might be expected, the sexual activities of the *devadasis* throughout India ranged from the coarse and vulgar to the sensitive and religiously dedicated.

Ritualism

Hindu popular religion abounds in ritualism. Whether worship takes place at home or in the temple, on pilgrimages or at festivals, or at other times and places, it is heavily involved with *kriyas* (rites) of various kinds. In the Brahmanas, for example, rites are assumed to be the most effective controlling agencies of the divine known to man. The assumption then and later gave a basis for the dominance of the brahmin caste in Indian life. In the Mimamsa philosophy, too, which recognized the importance of metaphysical abstractions, all that is good in the final analysis is governed by the faithful practice of ritual. Other writings and cults have stressed the primacy of ritual.

The core of Hindu ritual is the *puja* (adoration). It may be practiced at home or in the temple and it consists of a number of activities of a ritual nature. The exact number of these activities varies with the sects and local practices. Taken together they are called the *upachara*. Commonly they include attentions that are paid to the god who is being worshiped. One, for example, celebrates the daily awakening of the god. The god, like human beings, is assumed to sleep at night. In the morning preparations are made for his arousal. Whatever has been left from the previous day, such as flowers and sacrificial food, is taken away. The *garbhagriha* and the *vimana* are opened and aired through ceremonies. Other ceremonies seek to bring the god from his state of sleep. Sometimes the god takes a nap in the middle of the day and ceremonies are required at the beginning and the end of the nap period. Some of the major deities are believed to enter into long periods of hibernation or sleep, especially during the winter months, and similarly this fact is marked with special ceremonies. The ceremony of awakening is called *prabodha* for all these events. In addition to *prabodha,* the *puja* features other ceremonial activities throughout the day.

Hinduism is a many-faceted enterprise. It can scarcely be defined and delimited with logical categories. One of its chief features, however, is popular religion. Such religion varies greatly in itself, although it is focused upon such matters as worship in general, festivals, pilgrimages, the temples and the home, and various *kriyas* (rites). Collectively they illustrate a significant dimension of the religion, showing that Hinduism is a vital, practical faith which holds the allegiance of the masses in India.

SEVEN

The Person

Hinduism, like other complex religions and perhaps all religions, is concerned with a number of basic problems. One of these is the nature of the universe. Hinduism seeks to know what caused the world and how its ongoingness can be accounted for. It sets forth propositions regarding the constitution of the universe, its basic element or elements. It offers theories of nature. Religiously this concern is expressed in the belief in the gods and their responsibilities and activities. Hinduism, notwithstanding the developments of modern science as it relates to these matters, holds an essentially spiritual interpretation of the nature of the universe.

The nature of human community and history is a second problem with which Hinduism, like other religions, is concerned. Men find themselves in society from birth. The realization of this involvement comes with the earliest consciousness. Feral man can never be a mass phenomenon. Hinduism, then, is concerned with the nature of society. It seeks to provide rationales for the society that exists. It tries to make society more than mere happenstance. In fact, it relates society, as it does the universe, to spiritual principles, to the gods. This after all is what a religion does in contradistinction to scientific efforts, such as political science and sociology. Hinduism imputes religious meaning into the associational life of men.

A third concern of Hinduism, which is part and parcel of other religions as well, is for the nature of the person. The individual is everywhere a self-motivated concern. The possession of individuality and self-existence is ever a concern of persons. Personhood calls for explanation, and Hinduism seeks to provide insights on this subject too. It offers understanding regarding the place of the person in relation to other obvious centers of vitality, such as plants and animals. It charts the model course for human development, including education in the context of all of life's experiences. It proffers interpretations of some basic principles that undergird human behavior. All of these matters within Hinduism are viewed from an essentially religious standpoint. These basic concerns— the universe, society, and the individual—are not exclusive compartments. They are simply three conceptual pinnacles from which the landscape of a single terrain may be viewed.

Plant World

Hinduism holds that just about everything is infused with religious meaning. The person, his nature and destiny, can best be understood only in relation to the whole of the universe. Within that universe man is related to everything; he especially is a part of the created order, which also includes other living things such as plants and animals. First the plant world and then the animal world will be briefly examined in order that man himself may better be understood. The plant world is characterized by being *sthavara* or stationary and it includes herbs, plants, and trees. Like man, the plant world is a divine creation. The fertility of the soil and the necessity for water lead Hindus to think that these also are divine forces.

Elements of the botanical world were deemed to have potent characteristics even from the earliest times. For example, grasses of certain kinds played a part in Vedic ritual. Sacrificial offerings were placed upon grasses in the temple and a grass-strewn place was reserved so that the god could sit there. The priest and the *yajamana* (sacrificer) also sat on grasses. In the ceremony, moreover, one tuft of grass, called the *prastara,* was used to deceive the demons who might threaten the efficacy of the sacrifice. At a proper moment, when the demons had taken their place on the tuft, it was thrown into the sacrificial fire. But, following this, another blade of grass was also thrown into the fire in order to placate the demons. Sometimes, too, worshipers were required to wear grass clothes or to hold some grass in their hands as they held the sacred vessels. After the ceremony instruments were also wiped clean with grass. Aside from their use in the temple, grasses also were employed to construct the mat for meditation for the brahmin. The *darbha* is an especially popular kind of grass even today; it is used to make amulet rings and in offerings on particular days. When the *darbha* is used in an offering at an annual festival called *Darbha-ashtami,* it is potent enough to secure immortality for ten ancestors.

Hindu attitudes toward the coconut also illustrate the way in which the plant world has religious meaning and potency. Coconuts are believed to bring benefits beyond their use for food and drink. They are a symbol of fertility and are regularly presented to women who wish to conceive. They are viewed as a symbol of the human head and thus are offered in temple sacrifices. Even today in India ships are christened before launching by breaking a coconut on the ship's bow. Furthermore, the coconut as a symbol of a person's head has a surface with three distinct areas. These are said to represent Brahman, Vishnu, and Siva. Siva worship especially is associated with the coconut, and it is said that the three "eyes" of the coconut are symbolic of this three-eyed deity. In some places a coconut elaborately prepared with grasses, spices, flowers, coins, and the like is worshiped by the Saivites. Again, a special day is designated in July-August in which coconuts are thrown into the waters as offerings to the gods, accompanied by *mantras* and other festivities. This ceremony is said to cause the monsoon to mitigate its force, signalizing the possibility once again of engaging in coastal shipping.

Other parts of the botanical world, too many to be mentioned here in their entirety, are believed to have significance in Hinduism. The lotus (water-lily), for example, is the national flower of India and is regarded by many Hindus as a preeminent symbol of the religion, for it is said that the lotus, while being pure white in itself, is often a product of the dankest swamps. So, the believer in the midst of an evil world may become pure like the lotus. The two main types of fig tree, the banyan and the *pipal,* are held in high regard. It is claimed that Vishnu himself was born under the *pipal,* and regularly it is worshiped as an embodiment of that god. Under the *pipal* Gautama, the founder of Buddhism, received his enlightenment, and for many Indians the tree is a refuge for meditation. Its leaves are dried and powdered and used as medicine by many who suffer from a variety of complaints.

The *rudraksha* is another tree that is sacred in Hinduism. The seeds of its berries are made into rosaries by loyal Saivites, who think of the seeds as representing the third eye of Siva. Siva is also known as Rudra and the word *rudraksha* signifies Rudra's eye. One version of tradition has it that Rudra sheds these seeds as tears when he contemplates the fact that the world will finally be destroyed. The configuration of these seeds is thought to have special significance. A one-sided seed is very rare and is very valuable because such seeds are believed to bring satisfaction to every human wish. A two-faced seed represents the male and female principle and is valuable in certain rites, especially those involving sexuality. A three-sided seed represents the three main *lokas* (worlds). Seeds with a greater number of faces are each believed to have special significance as well. A six-sided seed, for example, represents the six philosophies of Hinduism, previously mentioned. Thus these aspects of the botanical world provide illustrations of the manner in which Hinduism infuses all herbs, plants, and trees with religious meaning and potency. The plant world is not dormant; it is vital. It serves man in human ways, such as the rice which is the staple diet of Indians. But it also has religious meaning for people and they increase their own welfare, both in this life and in the next, by the judicious employment of nature's products.

Animal World

The animal world, like the plant world, holds an important place in Hinduism. It constitutes another aspect of the created world and it is defined by being *jangama,* or moving, in its nature. Many of the scriptures and other writings of Hinduism describe this world and seek to provide an understanding of it. Animals thus are classified in various ways, although all of them are believed to have been created by the gods. Large animals, for instance, are classified in a threefold system. The *pasu* are the large domesticated animals, such as dogs, cows, sheep, pigs, and so forth. The *mriga* are the game animals, such as the gazelle and the deer. The *vyala* are the wild animals that constitute some threat to man in their native state, such as the tiger, the elephant, and the rhinoceros. Animals as moving things are also classified in other ways in the traditions of Hinduism: poisonous and nonpoisonous; whether they walk, swim, or fly; carnivorous or herbivorous; with bones or without; bloodless or with blood; according to their external features, hairy or feathered or with a shell; and living above or below the surface of the ground.

Animals are closely associated in Hinduism with the activities of the gods. The gods are associated with a *vahana* (vehicle) by which each is identified. Kama, the god of love, for example, is said to have a bowstring composed of bees which cause the sting of love in human beings. Vishnu appeared as a fish, tortoise, lion, and other animals in order to save the world from demons on various occasions. The conch shell, moreover, has a special place in Hinduism deriving from the belief that Krishna killed the sea demon Panchajana who had the form of a shell and lived in the deepest part of the ocean and then used the shell as a trumpet to announce his victory. From this and other legends the *sankha* (conch shell) is believed to have special properties and is blown in temple worship and on other auspicious occasions. This shell also is said to have sexual significance and women are presumably complimented if they are described with conch-shell attributes. *Kambustha* (shell-dwelling creatures), however, such as snails, molluscs, and crabs, among others, have been considered not fit for human consumption. Generally they are put in the sun to die, while their shells oftentimes are retrieved and used for ornamental and other purposes.

Some animals hold a very special place in Hinduism. The cow and its worship have been mentioned previously. The crocodile, for example, is often revered. It is the *vahana* of the river-goddess Ganga. Their presence in the Ganges sanctifies the water. Sometimes crocodiles are taken from the river and placed in tanks so that they can be fed and worshiped. Later they may be permitted to return to the river.

Elephants also are highly respected. They apparently were not known to the Aryans, but in time they became a prominent part of Hindu mythology. Their creation is told in several tales that reflect the marvel of men over such large creatures. Originally elephants are said to have been white and to have had wings. Most of them lost their whiteness and all of them lost their ability to fly when a branch upon which they were sitting broke and killed some students of a seer who in turn cursed them and brought about their present condition. A white elephant in India was well cared for and was not made to work; usually such an elephant was in the possession of the *raja* (ruler). The *mahout* (trainer) of elephants is a member of a particular professional class and the modes of training elephants are kept secret within the class. Elephants have traditionally been associated with royal life and processions. They were painted and clothed and in other ways ornamented. Their processional march was accompanied by festivities, including persons especially dressed for the occasion. In certain ways the products of the elephant have been thought to have magical potencies. Thus the sweat from the temples of an elephant, called *mada,* is an aphrodisiac. A woman unable to conceive is placed in elephant dung for about an hour and then is expected to have sexual relations with her husband in order to have a child. Men seeking to be more virile rub elephant urine on their foreheads.

Birds also play a part in Hinduism's concern with the animal world. The vulture, for example, was worshiped in early times, especially by the indigenous peoples in pre-Vedic times, and is thought to be in power in the third *loka,* the lowest region of the universe. The crow has a number of distinctions. It is carrier of three secrets. One is the secret of immortality; the crow is termed *chirajiva* (long-lived), a testimony to its power to survive. Another secret derives from its presence at the creation; it was created out of the then existing chaos. Lastly the crow holds the secret to hell, for it is believed to have dwelled there for ages of time. The crow is so respected that it is worshiped as a means of aiding ancestors who may be having difficulties in the afterlife. The *hamsa* (swan) also holds meaning. Usually white, it symbolizes like the lotus the possibility of being pure while existing in an impure world. It is able to live both in the water and on the land. In its ability to control its breathing it foretells the proper ways of breathing that characterize the saint who uses *pranayama* (breath control) as a yogic exercise.

Animals have played an important role in Hindu sacrifices from the earliest times. The horse in Vedic times was the subject of the *asvamedha* (horse sacrifice). The goat, the ram, and the cow also have been used. Animal sacrifices are still prevalent in connection with the worship of Durga and Kali. Animals to be sacrificed underwent a series of ceremonies. They were tied to the *yupa* (sacrifical post) outside the temple, which was prepared by the worshiper and his wife who spread *ghee* on the post. To the accompaniment of *mantras,* the animal was sprinkled with water on selected spots and dried, usually by the sacrificer's wife. Then, while the worshipers turned their faces away, the priest strangled the animal. The fat and meat of the animal were burned in homage to the gods and the blood was poured on the ground as a means of assuaging any gods who might be unhappy. In some times and places it was thought that the greater the suffering of the animal being sacrificed the greater the benefits to be derived. Sometimes, for example, a living animal would be cut up into a prescribed number of parts or it would be thrown from a height onto a spiked bed. Other animals would have their forelegs cut off and be left to die or would be split open so that the fetus could be removed from the living mother. It was claimed that such practices caught the attention of the gods, especially through the groans and moans of the sacrificed animals. But in a sense animals even in being sacrificed were a testimony to the significance which Hindus placed upon them.

The Person

The person as a self-conscious being has long been a subject of speculation and interpretation within Hinduism. The nature of personhood has been as intriguing and perplexing a subject as the nature of the starry heavens above. For Hinduism man's nature is a constant topic of investigation and concern. No simple or single interpretation has developed within the religion regarding the person, but in the main Hinduism has viewed man in diverse and imaginative ways. One of the persistent strands of interpreting the nature of the person is to view man as a microcosm. The person stands in contrast to the macrocosm, the universe or that which exists outside man. But man as a microcosm mirrors faithfully within himself that outer world. This means that Hinduism teaches in some of its important traditions that the person and

the universe are essentially one. As in the Upanishads and elsewhere, the Brahma and the *atman* are one. *Moksha* (salvation)
for the person consists of self-discipline to the point that this identity between self and the universe is maximized. One then is
delivered from the *maya* (illusion) of delimiting reality. The
atman (soul) is man's link to the divine. But even his body reflects
the nature of the world around him. His bodily fluids compare to
the waters of the rivers and seas, his bones compare to the earth
itself, and his breath to the air or wind. From this standpoint the
person and the universe are composed of the same elements; they
are bound by the same principles of activity, such as *karma*
(causality), and are together meaningful in the same way.

In the remainder of this chapter, including the discussion of the
nature of the mind, detailed information is provided merely for
the purpose of showing the complexity of Hindu thought on these
themes. As this is not the place for an exhaustive treatment of
these topics, they are given in a condensed form. They may be
read quickly or passed over entirely. They illustrate, perhaps above
all, the attention which has been given to such matters in Hindu
tradition and the kinds of solutions that have been proffered to
rather weighty questions.

The person's *atman,* a spiritual principle, is housed within the
sarira, or physical body. The *atman* is not free-ranging and is not
able to express itself in the main except within the context of the
sarira. The *sarira* is sometimes referred to as the *deha* (covering),
for it is assumed that the body covers or contains the *atman.*
Again, man in his earthly existence is spoken of as *dehin* (embodied), that is, he is not an ethereal creature, such as ghosts and
demons may be, but is sheathed with a bodily covering. In reality
the *sarira* itself is not a single entity, but consists of three parts,
each of which contains an *atman.* Each of these *atmans,* moreover,
is contained within one or more *kosas* (sheaths).

First, the *sthula-sarira* (the gross body) is the body that is
responsive to the senses of others. It is the visually evident body
of the person. This body is composed of five basic elements: air,

earth, ether, fire, and water. These *bhuta* (basic elements) are gathered together at conception to form the person, and at death they return to their original state. The *sthula-sarira* encloses the *bhutatman* (elemental self). It in turn is sheathed by the *annamaya-kosa* (food-made sheath). This *kosa* is so named because it is believed to be composed of the food which the person eats.

Second, the *linga-sarira* (sign body) contains the *jivatman* (soul of man). The *jivatman* is sheathed in a three-fold manner, each sheath relating to a sphere of meaning for the *jivatman*: ether, knowledge, and mind. The *linga-sarira,* moreover, also contains seventeen other features which constitute the perceiving self: five senses of perception, five modes of action, five vital forces, along with the *manas* (mind) and the *buddhi* (higher mind). The *sthula-sarira* and the *linga-sarira* are conjoined by *chakras* (points of energy) which supply vitality to the first body. The precise channels by which the *chakras* reach the *sthula-sarira* are termed the *nadis.* It is believed that more than eighty thousand *chakras* exist by which the *linga-sarira* motivates and stimulates the *sthula-sarira* into its observable actions. Certain occult aspects of Hinduism make much of the importance of the *chakras,* and it is claimed that a proper knowledge of them and their manipulation can be a source of effective functioning of the body itself and, therefore, of health for the person. For example, some occultists believe that it is possible to cure a toothache by massaging a particular rib. The *linga-sarira,* moreover, is not entirely destroyed when a person dies. A part of it survives death and forms the basis for the birth-death-rebirth cycle of human existence. The surviving part, however, is not eternal, for it returns to its original nature when the person attains *moksha* (final liberation).

Third, the *karana-sarira* (causal body) contains the *anandatman* (the bliss soul). This body is the arena of dreamless sleep and those states in which the self seems to transcend itself. The soul of this body is sheathed in a *kosa* which is bliss-formed. The actions of the *sthula-sarira* are recorded and stored in this body; in a sense it is the seat of *karma,* for it is this aspect of the person which continues after death, influencing and shaping the conditions of rebirth.

The *sthula-sarira* (gross body) is the object of detailed concern and study in Hinduism. Although the traditional understanding of anatomy was far from accurate in terms of modern knowledge, it did provide for descriptions of body parts and functions that were infused with religious connotations. The eye, for example, begins to function only upon birth, although all the other human organs are operative prior to birth. This insight has led Hindu sculptors to form the eye last in their creations. The eye is essentially a neutral organ in the sense that it naturally receives sense-data without input or evaluation. But the eye can become a source of meaningful communication. Thus the eye is able to benefit the person who looks upon auspicious persons and objects with a view toward securing a blessing. Similarly, if an enraged person casts a hateful glance at another individual, perhaps accompanied by a curse, the eye is able to create harm, both physical and spiritual. One, therefore, should avoid the so-called evil eye by averting one's glance. Children are instructed in the necessity of avoiding the evil eye. In the past children's faces about the eyes were colored black so that they could be protected.

The eye, moreover, is said to lose its functioning at the death of the person and so he goes sightless into the afterlife unless through a special ceremony he is granted the power to see even beyond death. Siva, of course, had a third eye which possessed such power that it could burn to ashes anything that aroused his anger. So some Hindus believe that each person has a latent third eye, located in the middle of the forehead, and that occultly it is a force for seeing even that which is obscured to the other two eyes.

Again, the orifices, or openings, of the body are thought to have special significance. It is recognized that there are internal and external orifices. All of these are called *kha*. Those which are exclusively external are termed *chhidras* (apertures). The *chhidras* are characterized by leakage and are thought of as the wet apertures. The human male has nine such *chhidras*: eyes, nose, mouth, ears, anus, and urethra. The *chhidras* also are connected with the intricate system of bodily fluids which are affected when leakages take place. So in the practice of certain occult exercises the *chhidras* must be blocked through the use of various *bandhas* (locks) and certain *asanas* (positions). By being seated and through the artful use of the fingers the occult practitioner is able to close the *chhidras* and thus preserve the essences of fluid that are related to desired goals. It is also believed that through self-discipline in prescribed ways these apertures may be blocked without the use of physical means, so that a self-disciplined person may not press his fingers to his ears and yet still not be able to hear outside sounds.

Mind

Hinduism is also concerned with the person's mental characteristics. Although it would probably not be fair to speak of Hinduism possessing a systematic psychology as this science has developed in the West, nevertheless the religion attributes to the person facilities and qualities that call that designation to mind. The total subject is too broad for treatment at this time, but the concept of the mind may be taken as illustrative of Hinduism's way of dealing with such matters. Actually Hinduism offers no strictly unified theory of the mind, but refers to the mind in a number of contexts without always making a coherence out of the several references. One aspect of the mind, for example, that which is associated with the ordinary mental activities of the person, is called *manas,* or the thinking faculties. The *manas* is the person's individual mind, the facilities of thought that he brings to bear upon ordinary activities of the common life. This is the meaning of the mind that includes *pratyaksha* (perception). It accounts for his *chetana* (awareness) that he is a person. It also consists of other attributes: *kalpana* (the ability to imagine), *chetas* (a low-order personal illumination), *chinta* (the capacity to handle thoughts), and *prayatna* (the ability to make decisions). The person also is able through these faculties to exercise a relatively high quality of personality, namely *chaitanya* (intelligence).

The individual's mind also is termed *ahamkara,* or the I-maker. This connotation refers broadly to the ego-conscious features of the person. It is this aspect of the self that reflects the distinctive personality of the individual who is formed by fragments of culture. What is appropriated by the five senses and reasoned about in the *manas* sense is then formed into the changing person by the *ahamkara.* This aspect of the person, moreover, is quite capable of distortion of reality. This distortion is evidenced by the fact that everyone is distinctive and holds only a part of the total truth or reality. Error, for example, may be due to the inadequate functioning of the perceptive aspect of the *manas.* That would be a malfunctioning of the *manas* and is everyone's possibility. But the *ahamkara* is capable of more than this kind of error. It is prone to deal selectively with the facts obtained through perception in the interests of the self. Yet the *manas* maintains a counteracting element, the *antah-karana* (inner mind). Sometimes the seat of this function is said to be in the heart or the heart itself. It is the capacity of the mind to look deeply within the self and in some moral and corrective sense to determine when the *ahamkara* is cheating and to influence the self to think and act in a proper manner. In a word, the *antah-karana* comes close to the notion of the conscience. With the meaning of conscience the *antah-karana* is spoken of as the *antar-yamin* (inner guide). It forms the basis for the judgment that *dosha* (sin) has taken place, and with the existence of sin the development and action of *karma* is grounded.

The individual's mind, however, is not unique or autonomous. In addition to the mind of the person there are other aspects of mind in the universe. In fact, Brahma also is mind. Brahma represents the universal and transcendental aspects of mind. Brahma's mind, however, is not formed through the ordinary processes, such as perception, so necessary to man. Brahma's mind is self-formed and is not dependent upon any element beyond itself. It is altogether perfect and in most interpretations does not fall under the limits ascribed to the person's *ahamkara* or any other human attribute that might in itself cause Brahma's mind to be less than wholly perfect. Brahma, the universal mind, knows each and every facet of truth and reality in itself, but he also knows everything in its totality. What he knows, moreover, he knows without any distortion. So the person takes Brahma as his model and seeks always to fashion his thinking according to the sublime attributes of Brahma.

Between the mind of the person and the mind of Brahma stand some other aspects of mind. This middle range of mind consists of the knowledge, intelligence, corporate abilities and skills, reliable culture, and other attributes which generally exist. This kind of mind is not delimited as is the mind of the person who to a marked degree is dependent upon it for the content of his own mind. Again, it is not Brahma's mind, for often it falls quite short of perfection. But it does exist and it does possess clearly mental characteristics. Hindus sometimes refer to this mind as *chitta,* or knowing in its universal sense. At other times *chitta* is employed, as in the Yoga philosophy, to refer to certain aspects of the individual's mind and comes close in meaning to the *chetas* of the *manas.*

Another term which bridges the gap between the mind of the person and both universal knowing and the mind of Brahma is *buddhi* (wisdom). *Buddhi* signifies one of the personalized manifestations of the *chitta.* It also represents the highest form of human consciousness. It connotes the enlightened person, the illumined individual, that one who possesses not only knowledge but right knowledge, not only perception but compelling insight, not only a mass of facts but coherent thought. Thus the mind in Hinduism is a complex set of concepts and definitions, ranging from the innermost aspects of the person's mental life to the farthest reaches of the cosmos, that is, to Brahma himself.

The person in Hinduism, in sum, is a complex entity consisting of body, mind, and soul. These elements of the person are complex in themselves and at many points defy neat analysis. But the person also is a single self. All the component parts are brought together in a particular individual. Individuals, moreover, are self-directing, that is, they relate themselves to goals in life. The effort to fashion behavior in terms of these goals is a principal duty of the person. Being goal-oriented, persons are dynamic in their behavior. They are changeable and flexible. They are able to harness their component parts in efforts to become what they have accepted for themselves as model persons. Some sense of the ideal person, then, is apparent in Hinduism. Life is directed toward becoming a model individual.

Models

The model person in Hinduism, however, does not fit a single description. Every Hindu has the possibility of distinctive development. Yet from a generalized perspective a number of models are available. In the previous chapter, for example, a number of religious professions were mentioned, such as the priest, the guru, the swami, the *sadhu,* the yogi, the *sannyasin,* the astrologer, the pandit, and others. For the religiously inclined these constitute models for personal achievement. They in fact do appeal to sizable numbers of persons, although they obviously do not embrace a large portion of the total Indian population.

Another model for emulation in the Hindu tradition is epitomized by persons, both human and divine, portrayed in historical writings of the religion. In this regard the Bhagavad Gita provides an apt example. In this work Krishna appears as an admirable character. In addition, Arjuna, with whom Krishna enters into dialogue, also is offered as a model person. Krishna and Arjuna embody three ideals conjoined in one person. First, they are warriors. They show the virtues of manliness. They are unafraid of enemies. They are eager to take up the cause of the weak and less fortunate. In battle they do not waver; their courage is their strength and the instrument of their victories. Second, they are scholars. Krishna and Arjuna engage in rather sophisticated reasonings about the nature of the world around them and of the proper course of human conduct. They are reflective persons who do not act without thought regarding motives and means. Third, they are lovers. They are young and physically attractive to members of the opposite sex. They engage in those activities which are assumed to be admired by women. In sexual activities they are proficient and by their dash and daring are able to attract a variety of women.

The model of the lover is highly developed in Hinduism. The Kamasastras are writings that are devoted to the nature and skills of love; Kama is the god of love. In these and other erotic writings the requirements of successful loving are described. Men and women are classified physically according to body types, including the characteristics of their *linga* and *yoni*. Consideration also is given to the intersexual mixing of these types of persons. The ideal lover is portrayed in a number of Hindu documents. One such hero is the legendary Udayana, who is said to be the son of Sahasranika, a king. The young and attractive prince, Udayana, appears as a Don Juan in Indian garb, being irresistible to women. One princess, for example, falls in love with him merely by looking at him. Another falls in love with him by simply viewing his portrait. Yet another falls in love with him only by hearing his name. In action the suave, skilled-in-the-arts, physically appealing Udayana becomes everyman's hero in love-making. In the practice of many Hindus, however, the somewhat romantic and idealized lover-model of Udayana was not always achieved. The *nagaraka,* or town man, of the fifth century A.D., for example, was more of a degenerate dandy for whom self-adulation and the venal use of sexuality were prime limitations.

Two other models for personal development also are offered by Hinduism. One of these, caste, is not merely a voluntarily accepted definition of the self in action, but is in fact a social system which binds most Hindus. Theoretically the caste system provides for four essential modes of personal existence, modeled after the four main caste divisions: the brahmin, the *kshattriya,* the *vaisya,* and the *sudra.* These correspond to the priest, the warrior, the artisan, and the unskilled. Of course, this model is very complex in all of its details and will be discussed as a separate topic in the next chapter. The other model is that of the *asramas,* or stages of life. Somewhat theoretically also Hinduism provides for four stages of personal growth which carry a person from birth to death. The *asramas* will be described in the final chapter of this book.

Motives

Hinduism also maintains another and somewhat different set of interpretations of the desirable goals of life. These are related less to socially organized forms, such as caste; they pertain fundamentally to the motives of the person or the individual's inner dynamics. They seek to interpret the drives which stimulate and direct persons toward action and social objectives. By admitting four basic motives, Hinduism acknowledges that all men are not motivated by a single drive and that a complex understanding of the differences among individuals is most suited to the actual conditions of human behavior. The first two motives are based upon self-expression and in general represent sanctioned but less desirable motives for conduct. The first motive is *kama* (love). Love from this standpoint is broadly interpreted as pleasure. Hinduism notes that many persons are legitimately devoted to their own pleasure. The religion does not look askance at persons who seek to maximize their own pleasure, for this motive is not contrived; rather, it is natural. Men seek to avoid pain at almost all costs and they are attracted to those modes of conduct that will provide them with the greatest pleasure. The motive for pleasure, moreover, need not go unattended as though every person has a sound sense of how his own pleasure may be secured. Pleasure is a suitable subject for study and for personal development. Thus books exist within Hinduism which teach how the person seeking pleasure may develop his capacity and effectiveness.

The second motive is *artha* (power). Hinduism acknowledges that the drive for success motivates many persons. The individual is not to be condemned if he chooses to become powerful. Power in itself is not a negative value. It may be sought for purely personal ends and if it is so sought it is legitimate. But power also may be sought for socially constructive purposes. The man of power may bring immense benefits to others. A positive blending of personal and social motives are joined in this motive.

Pleasure and power, however, are highly self-centered motives. They are aimed chiefly at satisfying the person's desires. These desired goals are natural in the sense that they are embodied in every person's character. As such they are not to be demeaned. Yet they often do not lead to true and lasting satisfaction for the individual. Persons who follow them are often frustrated. The pleasure and power that are attained are found to be shallow and jading. Again, the goals of pleasure and power in the final analysis are unstable. The pleasure of today may become the sorrow of tomorrow. The power of today may be the powerlessness of tomorrow. Also, these two motives are insatiable; they never reach a point at which the person may rest with complete satisfaction. So two other motives are acknowledged. These are higher in that they overcome to an appreciable degree the deficiencies of both pleasure and power. They rest, moreover, not upon self-expression, but upon self-denial. They are grounded not on personal desire, but upon the suppression of desire.

The first of the two higher motives is based upon *dharma*, or the moral and religious law. The person who is guided by this motive does not seek his own satisfactions. Quite the contrary, this individual restrains his own pleasure by doing his duty. Duty operates on principles which are not self-serving. The irascible principle rests upon what is good for one and for others without regard for what one may desire for one's own gain. Legalistic Hinduism supplies an ample and well-detailed description of how the person seeking to fulfill the *dharma* way of life should behave.

The second of the two higher motives is based upon *moksha*, or salvation. This is the highest motive of all and it depends upon the complete renunciation of the self. All the satisfactions of the other motives are fragmentary and impermanent. The self is still bound by the limitations of human existence, especially those of birth, death, and rebirth. *Moksha* looks to the breaking of this ongoing cycle and to the attainment of a truly blissful state that is devoid of all human and worldly imperfections. *Moksha*, then, is the preeminent motive for living, for through it the individual achieves supreme satisfaction.

Margas

The fourfold understanding of persons' motives is based upon a gradient interpretation of conduct or styles of life. It is assumed that individuals will find themselves acting mainly within the context of one of the four. All are sanctioned, yet there is a lowest and a highest. Changes in a person's fundamental orientation to himself and to others may and do occur, but chiefly an individual's lifetime is characterized by one type of motive. It is vaguely hoped that a person may ascend in the order from one life to another. Yet each person in life follows one *marga* (path), which, while held in common with others, is distinctly his own. The *marga* connotes a pattern of life, a consistent way of doing things, a set of stages by which one seeks to attain one's objective. The *marga* of a person may pertain to any of the four motives, but in general it is related to the goal of *moksha*. *Margas* have been differentiated in Hinduism and described in some detail in the several religious writings. They also take form within various sects and other movements as key features of the religious quest for salvation. Several of the many *margas* may be noted for illustrative purposes. The *karma-marga* is the path of good works. It mainly relates to the *dharma*, or religious and moral code incumbent upon the believer. In this roadway the person seeks salvation by doing his duty without fear or favor. He strives to be faithful in his obligations to himself, his family, and his community. The *kriya-marga* concentrates upon action. The believer practices the rituals, takes part in temple worship, is concerned with the proper making and installing of idols, and in ordinary affairs seeks to act from a religious orientation. The *jnana-marga* stresses right knowledge. It suggests that salvation is attained through proper reasoning and belief. Existence is *maya*, illusionary, and the primary way of escaping from error is by right thinking. This *marga* has appeal to those Hindus who base their religion on philosophic considerations. The *bhakti-marga* offers the path of personal devotion to a personal deity. It emphasizes the preeminence of faith as the means by which transcending reality is reached. Salvation is found through worshipful acts of devotion and adoration. In addition to these, other *margas* are characterized by other traits. There are *margas* which stress the pathway of physical culture, as in the Yoga philosophy, or the virtue of nonaction in the belief that all action suffers from imperfections, or the notion that god is within the believer and simply needs to be recognized in the ways in which his grace is displayed in the individual. While these various *margas* are available as particular paths for the attainment of one's goals, especially for the achievement of *moksha*, they also may be practiced or followed in combination. Many Hindus believe that no one *marga* will exclusively bring one to the final state of salvation, so that they take two or more as particularly suited to their own needs and insights.

Historically Hinduism has responded to several basic human concerns. One of these is man's concern for himself. Individuals everywhere are concerned with the nature of the universe and the principles underlying collective behavior. But they also and to a marked degree have been intensely interested in questions of self-definition. They wish to know who they are. Hinduism offers a complex explanation of the nature of the individual, seeing him as a part of the created order, along with the plant and animal worlds.

The person, moreover, is in himself a complex entity whose diversity and mystery often elude human efforts. The person, however, is not completely understood simply in terms of his basic nature, but must be fully known through the goals which he takes to guide his conduct. Even these goals are complex and no single aim in life is suited to all persons. The individual must seek his own salvation by following a path in which his motives are satisfied. Salvation is the final and immutable goal for all human beings, but the ways by which it can be attained are manifold. In this life, moreover, it is realistic to understand that various persons are in various stages toward the achieving of that final goal.

EIGHT

Society

Men everywhere find themselves in community. To be human, almost by definition means to live an associational life with other human beings. Yet the nature of community is one of the seemingly universal and perennial questions that confronts persons. In Hinduism as elsewhere men have wondered about the origins of society. They have envisaged a time and circumstance in which perhaps the binding or political aspects of the community were not needed. They have explored the relation between the existence of the community, especially in its origins, and the activities of the gods. They have been concerned regarding the proper organization of the community, giving thought as to what form or forms of leadership and control are most beneficial. Beyond political leadership, they have sought to account for the apparent social and economic differences among persons that society reflects and enforces. Differences in individual capacities, interests, and skills also must be reasoned about. Finally, consideration is given to ethical subjects, for in them the relationships between the person and others is formulated and codified. All of these questions and more have been asked in the long course of Hinduism's history, and to them a variety of answers has been given. In Hinduism such inquiries and their responses may be thought to relate to the subjects of government, social organization or caste, and ethics. With no thought of being comprehensive or definitive, these subjects comprise for the present purposes the teachings of Hinduism on society.

The teachings of Hinduism on the nature of government are referred to as *nitisastra*, or welfare teachings. In this context politics is not only the art of governing but also includes economics, ethics, and other matters. For example, it commonly is not possible within the Hindu tradition to separate politics from economics. The way in which a state is governed is thought necessarily to bear a close relationship to trade, production, and agriculture. Similarly, the functioning of government is assumed to be inseparable from the economic basis of support for the society. So, too, with all the elements of men's social relationships; they all fit a pattern of vital relationship in which the parts cannot be understood and manipulated independently. Taken together they represent a system of interlocking relationships, each being dependent upon all the others for its meaning and success.

The dominance of the *raja*, or king, in Indian history is the central fact of its traditional government. But other forms also have existed. In various times and places, from the earliest days until quite recently, tribes have existed which have not been ruled by monarchies. These have been more simple units of human community in which often a tribal chief maintained more than a ruling function. The chief included within his responsibilities most if not all of the interlocking relationships that comprise society in its totality. The chief, moreover, was not an autocratic *raja* who ruled in sovereign fashion. Rather, the chief tended to be the head of a tribal community in which familial relationships were determining. His position usually was not only the result of his birth, but a consequence of oligarchical arrangements in which he was more like a tribal father than a *raja*. Commonly a family council was the practical determiner of the course of events within the community.

Kingship

Kingship, however, has been the prevalent model for government in Hinduism. It was not the original state of affairs, however, for originally both the gods and men enjoyed an idyllic life in which they were able to regulate their social relationships through self-control and by the application of universally accepted ethical principles. The gods themselves in the beginning had no kings, but the *asuras* (demons) took advantage of this condition and, according to the Brahmanas, waged battle against the gods, often defeating them. The gods then saw the necessity for kings; the *asuras* had kings. The gods met their dilemma by appointing Indra as their ruler. Thereafter they were able to withstand the *asuras* with some success. The rise of kingship among men followed a similar pattern. Men originally were good and had no need for an agent of control in society. In time, however, the golden age dimmed; men became selfish and immoral. This was the period of the *matsyanyaya*, or fish logic, in which the larger fish or stronger men ate the smaller fish or men. Kingship became necessary. Men appealed to Brahman for a ruler and he appointed Manu, a law codifier shrouded by both antiquity and myth, who with some reluctance accepted and composed the Laws of Manu, a *smriti* scripture of Hinduism, in which the proper relationships among men were defined and described. The laws include many subjects: cosmology, rites and ceremonies, dietary restrictions, the duties of kings, the *asramas*, and rules of morality, among other topics. But its main contribution is its sanctioning of the caste system, with the brahmin caste as the chief interpreter and enforcer of the system, a view which has traditionally been criticized by nonbrahmins. Other writings in Hinduism also comment on kingship. The Atharva Veda, for example, provides information on the subject. The Aitareya Brahmana details how a king should be crowned. The epic tales, the Mahabharata and the Ramayana, moreover, exalt kingship in their stories of heroism.

Great homage was accorded to the *raja*. It was believed that his welfare was intimately bound up with the welfare of his people. A just and good king not only was reflected in the character of his people; he also brought about sweeter honey, more abundant crops, and rain. According to the Ramayana, however, a bad king has the opposite effect. An evil king creates discord among his people, and sons will not obey their parents. But a bad king also affects nature, so that the rain does not fall, the crops are meager, and springs do not give sweet water. From this standpoint it was desirable that good kings rule and that they be given every sign, both material and symbolic, of the support of their people.

The *rajas* also were associated with divinity. Their *rajasuya* (coronation) was a year-long, elaborate ceremony which corresponded to the investiture of Indra as king of the gods. The king's being was thus imbued with divine characteristics, and magical powers were said to result. From time to time these powers were further revitalized through other ceremonies. One of these was the *vajapeya,* or vigor draught, in which cups of *soma* wine were drunk. The number seventeen recurs throughout the ceremony. There were seventeen participants, seventeen animals originally were sacrificed, seventeen chants were sung, and seventeen invocations offered. The *rajas,* moreover, were accorded designations that increased their stature. Instead of *raja* (ruler), they became *maharaja* (great ruler), or *bhupati* (earth ruler), or *bhupala* (earth guardian). Also, the *raja* was called *rajadhiraja* (king of kings) and *maharajadhiraja* (great king of kings). Sometimes they were even addressed directly by terms that referred to the gods themselves.

The kings, however, had a hard role to fulfill. Basically they expressed three important qualities: *prabhava* (majesty), *utsaha* (energy), and *mantra* (wisdom). These three attributes were required of the good king and any diminution of them in practice led those around him and his people to be critical of him. A king who could not maintain these qualities, especially by reason of age, could resign in favor of his oldest son. He then might kill himself or simply leave his palace to spend his remaining days as a forest hermit. Again, the inadequate king ran the danger of revolt. The Mahabharata, for example, says that revolution against such a king is proper and that a king who fails to protect his people and causes them not to prosper should be killed even as a mad dog is slain. Such action on the part of the people, however, should not be lightly entertained, for a king of any description is better than no king at all.

In practice the king depended upon others for his successful functioning. Usually he maintained an advisory council of between seven and thirty-five persons. The council was chaired by a *mahamantrin*, or prime minister. This chief minister was responsible for the actual running of the government and there are many examples in Indian history where he was the *de facto* ruler also. Oftentimes, moreover, the *mahamantrin*'s office became hereditary, which strengthened the authority of the position. The king also depended upon other aides. The *gehapati*, or house lord, was the chamberlain responsible for the operations of the king's palace and possessions. The *senapati*, or general, was his commander-in-chief for his armed forces. The *samnidhatri*, or treasurer, held responsibility for the king's finances and that of the kingdom. The *pradvivaka*, or problem-decider, played the role of the chief judge. In addition, the king depended upon charioteers, bards, physicians, astrologers, artists, and others.

Although the king relied on many functionaries to maintain his responsibilities, he usually was not a remote or unapproachable person. Often he was accessible to his people, who came to him with their problems and disputes so that he personally could settle them. He spent time almost daily in receiving dignitaries from other kingdoms, both far and near. Also, he depended upon a number of princes or viceroys, usually of his own family, who were stationed in the provinces to maintain the king's government. In addition, the king himself went from place to place, usually accompanied with pomp and circumstance, in order to be seen and to be available to his people.

The king also had a female entourage. Its size was an indication of his position and wealth. The *mahishi*, or chief wife, of the king often wielded considerable influence with the king and with others, and at times she was the real power behind the throne. She managed the female sector of the palace and on ceremonial occasions had an important role to play. The *mahishi* was usually of royal blood, the daughter of a neighboring *raja* with whom the king wished for amicable relations. In addition to the *mahishi* the king had other wives. Some of these could be chosen from the royal families of allies, others could result from the spoils of war, and others were taken from his own people, even of the lowest castes, because of their beauty or other talents. It was the eldest son of the *mahishi*, sometimes called the *yuvaraja* or minor king, who was the heir-apparent.

The king, in Hinduism, was a personal ruler whose duties were fulfilled through other persons. But the king and his associates were not whimsical, subjective, and arbitrary in their actions. The king had his *rajaniti* (kingcraft) in which certain principles of governing were explicated. He also was guided by *pranayana*, or administrative policy. In addition, *dandaniti*, or rod-policy, covered the manner in which force should be employed. In these and other ways a set of norms and procedures were available to the king for the administration of the government. These guides were available in a variety of documents, some of which have already been mentioned. Perhaps the most significant work on political administration, however, is the Arthasastra, which is attributed to Kautilya, who was believed to be the minister to Chandragutpa Maurya (320-297 B.C.), a ruler in one of the great dynastic lines of India. This document, only discovered at the beginning of this century, provides information on the control of the state, the way in which the economy should be used to maintain and increase power, and the waging of war. It is an exercise in practical politics, a hand-book on the methods by which the king can succeed. The Artha-sastra has been compared with the political views of Niccolo Machiavelli (A.D. 1469-1527), the Italian statesman and writer on government, in that it at points places expediency above public morality.

From the Arthasastra and other documents the nature of Hindu statecraft becomes apparent. Thus effective rulership is said to depend upon seven *prakriti*, or elements. First, the *raja* stands at the pinnacle of the political order and is ultimately responsible for everything. Second, his *amatyas*, or ministers, are necessary adjuncts to the exercise of the *raja*'s power. Third, *durgas*, or forts, are necessary so that the security of the nation may be maintained, by the actual use of force if necessary. Fourth, a *rashtra*, or na-tional territory, is required and the constant preservation of it is a basic obligation of the king and others. Fifth, the *kosa*, or treasury, secured by detailed rules of taxation, is indispensable to the other elements. Sixth, the *bala*, or army, is required so that affronts from external enemies may be thwarted. Seventh, *mitra*, or allies, are a fundamental requirement, for no matter how strong a king and nation may be, it must look to other states that are sympathetic to it and which will support it forcefully in times of war. All of these *prakriti* taken together and held in balance con-stitute the features of government to which the king and others must give constant attention. By being proficient in each and all of them, the health of the state is preserved and enhanced.

Each of the *prakriti* constitutes a basis for detailed analysis and prescription. The *mitra*, for example, is subdivided into a number of kinds and qualities. A king needs to be aware of the kinds of states that surround him. Some states are openly enemy states and are, therefore, dangerous. Such are the prime bases for war. Other states are openly friendly and everything should be done to keep them in that condition. Friendly states also have friendly states related to them and these also must be kept in mind. Some states are essentially neutral and will give their support to either side in the case of war. A combination of efforts may be useful in dealing with them: blandishment and threat. Other states are strong and secure. They constitute generally no cause for alarm, for their rulers are often not covetous of other states' territories. Yet other states are the friends of the enemies of a state and so comprise a danger. By this scheme the king and his associates were able to chart the kingdom's *mitra* relationships.

Similarly, the kinds of relations between states needs to be further viewed from the perspective of the quality of state relations. Hindu teachings stress six qualities: peace, war, neutrality, preparedness, alliance, and duplicity. The wise and strong king, then, should rely on an understanding in detail of both the kinds and the qualities of his relations with other states. These relations, moreover, are dynamic and require constant review and adaptation. Ongoing relations between states were maintained by *dutas* (ambassadors). These were of various kinds. Some were plenipotentiaries who negotiated with the full powers of the *raja*; others were envoys who were sent merely to deliver a message. Still others were ambassadors who worked under strict instructions from the home government.

Villages

In Indian villages, in the past and now, the panoply of kingly government was not evident and democratic government was more apparent. Villages were administered by a *panchayat*, or village council. This council was further administered by five *panchas* (officials) who almost daily were available to settle matters of taxation, caste disputes, family quarrels, and other problems of the village. Problems that existed between villages were referred to a *parishad*, or assembly of learned men of whom three or more were required to be highly versed in Hindu traditions and skilled in making sound decisions. On occasion the heads of the village councils would meet, and such a body was called a *sabha*. Beyond these forms of village government was the *samiti*, a popular assembly in which many persons participated, including the higher governmental officials. Usually the *samitis* had a social as well as a political function; they were effective instruments for the establishment of broad social solidarity.

Caste

A very special feature of Indian life, enforced by Hinduism, is caste. Actually the word is not Indian; it is derived from the Portuguese word, *casta*, for race, breed, or kind. No one word for caste exists in the native languages in India, although the existence of caste is almost everywhere recognized and followed. So pervasive is caste that it not only embraces Hindus but also influences some Muslim, Christian, and other groups as well. Despite its importance in Indian society, no one knows for sure how it originated. Mythologically it is said not to have existed at the beginning of human time. Then everyone belonged to the same class. This was at the time of the *krita–yuga,* or first age. The whole class or caste was called the *hamsa.* But in the following ages mankind deteriorated and immorality increased, so that in various successive ages the several castes came into existence. The brahmins, it is said, still retain some of the traces of their being derived from the *hamsa.*

Another version of the origins of caste points to the Rig Veda hymn, the Purusha-sukta, the nineteenth hymn and the twelfth verse in Mandala X, which is thought by some scholars to be a late interpolation. This verse says that the castes were divinely created. Here the fourfold division of society is related to the physical features of Purusha. The brahmin was the god's mouth, the *kshattriya* was his arms, the *vaisya* was his thighs, and the *sudra* was his feet. This verse is remarkable for many reasons, but among them is the fact that it is very often quoted, especially by high-caste Hindus, and also by reason of the further fact that the verse's sentiment has been taken with gross variations as a divinely prescribed sanction of a social system for a nation of great population which is without parallel in human history. In addition to this verse, however, there exist in Hinduism a number of important documents which also reinforce the primacy of the caste arrangements. One of these, of course, is the Brahmanas in which priestly religion with its heavy emphasis on ritual is offered as the true faith. Again, the Laws of Manu in great detail analyzed and codified the plethora of rules and regulations that pertain to most of the varied aspects of caste. Probably the idea of the fourfold division of society as an archetype was largely the creation of the composer of the laws, although obviously the writer of the laws also was influenced by accounts of caste already existing in his time and previously.

Many theories exist that seek to explain the origins of caste in India on a nonreligious basis, but these are in nature more suggestive than conclusive. One theory suggests that conquest and *varna,* or color of skin, account for caste. It is asserted that the Aryan invaders were dominantly lighter skinned than the indigenous peoples and that the caste system reflects the divinely based social rationale by which the conquerors assigned persons in the new society. The Aryans became the top three castes, while the conquered became the fourth, or *sudra,* caste. But there are drawbacks to this theory. A brahmin, for example, may generally be of lighter skin, yet even a jet-black brahmin is a brahmin. His caste is not determined solely by his color. Again, the Aryans seem not to have dominated the east and south of India, yet in those places the caste system is quite strong, suggesting perhaps that it did not have an exclusively Aryan base.

Another theory proposes that caste derived from certain occupational distinctions that arose early in Indian history. According to the Laws of Manu, each caste has specialized responsibilities: the brahmin studies, teaches, sacrifices, gives and receives gifts; the *kshattriya* protects the people, sacrifices, and studies; the *vaisya* studies and sacrifices, but he also tills the soil, breeds cattle, trades, and lends money; and the *sudra* has only the duty of serving the three higher castes. The subdivisions within each caste, moreover, tend to reinforce this theory, for to a very large extent they are based on occupational distinctions. Yet this theory too has its deficiencies. Agriculture, for example, is an occupation that is widely practiced by members of several castes. A number of castes have priests who are not brahmins. The more narrow definition of the duties of the *kshattriya*, or warrior caste, has largely disappeared. Many government workers are not members of this caste, nor are many members of the armed forces. This theory, then, like many others is partially helpful in explaining the origins of caste, but it cannot be pressed too hard. Probably a combination of factors best accounts for the rise of caste, although the precise relationship of them to each other is lost in the vagaries of antiquity.

The fourfold caste division of Indian society has historically been mainly an ideal. There have been times when it has been realized to greater and less degrees. Usually it recalls what the original state of society was supposed to be after the period of the *hamsa*. At times it is taken as a ready reference to a simple classification of many existing groups that hold a place in the caste system. But the fourfold division in reality is supplanted by a much more complex system in which a large number of castes and subcastes are found. No one knows with surety the exact number of castes and subcastes at the present time. Some authorities say that there are as many as three thousand castes and more than 25,000 subcastes. The numbers offered largely depend upon personal judgment and definition. Both the castes and the subcastes, however, possess the same characteristics.

No matter how it originated, caste in India's long history and even today is an indisputable fact. It is probably the most significant influence upon individual and collective behavior. While its influence is great, it is difficult to encompass within exception-proof categories. Yet some of its basic characteristics may be outlined with a certain assurance that they are common features of the social system. First, the caste system is endogamous. Perhaps most basically it provides for groups of families in which the members can marry each other. This means that the system is hereditary in that a person's place in society is determined not by his own efforts but, rather, by the place of his parents. In general it means that one cannot marry up, that is, use marriage as a device for social climbing. Thus the caste system has maintained a kind and degree of social stability for India which is remarkable. Second, caste is marked by commensality. This restriction signifies that food may be received from and eaten in the presence of members of the same caste or a higher caste. Sometimes this limit is spoken of as a prohibition against interdining. Members of different castes are regulated not only in the social experience of eating, but in other social relationships. It restricts the distances which various castes are required to maintain from other castes. For example, a member of one subcaste may be required to remain thirty-six paces from a brahmin and only twelve from a member of another subcaste. Where distances are difficult to keep, such as in a teeming metropolitan area, the restriction against members of different castes physically touching each other may still be retained.

Third, caste to a large extent holds to work exclusiveness. Each caste and subcaste is characterized by a particular vocational basis. Each caste member assumes the work of his caste. Over many years the caste specialization of work has led to a fairly traditional form of economy in which the interests and the skills of the father are passed to the son without regard to the overall social needs. But it also has led to highly developed skills within accepted occupations, for the generations have been able to inculcate the young in the family regarding techniques of production that otherwise might be lost.

Fourth, caste is characterized by hierarchical relationships among the several castes. The castes and their subcastes are not equally regarded; each holds a position of social regard in relation to the others. So the members of a subcaste will in general be well aware of the position of their subcaste in relation to the other subcastes around them. They will know whether their subcaste is inferior, superior, or equal to another subcaste. The *sonar* (goldsmith), in this arrangement, is superior to the *sutar* (carpenter). The *sutar*, on the other hand, is superior to the *goala* (milkman) even as the latter is superior to the *teli* (oil merchant).

In addition to these four basic characteristics of caste, other points of distinction also hold to a greater or less degree. Traditionally, for example, the three highest castes are said to be twice-born. They are born first at birth, but they are born a second time when they complete a ceremony in youth in which they are invested with their special standing. As twice-born persons they are entitled to study the Vedas, perform sacrifices, and enter into the *asramas*, or formal stages of life-development. The *sudra*, or lowest caste member, is only once–born and he is not permitted the privileges of the others. Theoretically the castes are also differentiated on the basis of certain external expressions. Each caste has its own distinctive color: white for the brahmin, red for the *kshattriya*, yellow for the *vaisya*, and black for the *sudra*. Caste members use these colors for their dress or for some ornamentation of their dress and for their homes. A number of religious elements also distinguish the castes. While the *sudra* has virtually none, the other castes have special times for family ceremonies, ages when they begin their religious studies, special festivals, and so forth. In the twice-born ceremony, for example, the brahmin is invested with a thread of a special grass, the *kshattriya* with a bow-string, and the *vaisya* with wool or hemp. Sometimes in the villages the well from which the villagers gather water may be the focus of distinction. Caste members may all be able to draw water from a well, while nonmembers or outcastes may be prohibited. In some cases, where only one well is available, members of the castes may draw from one side of the well and nonmembers from the other side. One's relationship, then, to the use of a well may reflect one's caste membership.

Each caste or subcaste has a high degree of self-awareness and enforces its own requirements through a caste council. Questions that may arise regarding caste membership, especially through the presentation of new or exceptional circumstances, are settled by the council. The individual member of a caste or subcaste is guided by his own conscience and by well-known and well-enforced standards for behavior. The dangers of contamination from relations with other castes in general is the concern of a superior caste in relationship to an inferior one. But at times, even inferior castes are deeply resentful of being polluted by relationships with superior ones. It has been known, for example, that members of outcaste groups have punished even brahmins who have strayed into their living quarters.

The fourfold division of society into castes has been and is more of a theory than a reality. The theory, supported by such teachings as the Laws of Manu, was that almost everyone fell into one of the four castes. Of course, there were the *mlechchhas*, or foreigners. They were not Hindus in the first place. They did not acknowledge the Vedas, the validity of the brahminical system, and the other attributes of Hinduism. The foreigners were essentially barbarians who were beneath the dignity of even the *sudras*. In early times the *mlechchhas* included the Greeks and Persians, among others, and in later times included Muslims and Europeans. These had no place in the caste system.

Those persons and groups that did not fit into the fourfold caste system were designated as members of the *panchama*, or fifth caste. In actuality, however, considerable resistance to the use of this designation has existed because it seems to infer that in reality there are five rather than four castes. The pious Hindu would deny this, insisting that there can be only four. Other terms, then, have been employed to refer to the *panchamas*, such as outcastes, untouchables, depressed classes, and scheduled castes.

The *panchamas* include more than barbarians. They also consist of a number of tribes that usually are not of Aryan descent. These tribes often are still primitive and inhabit various unsettled areas in India. Often they take their names from their place of habitation and are associated with particular means of subsistence, such as hunting or coconut-growing. A few are not primitive and have developed considerable pride in themselves as well as worthwhile cultural contributions. In Vedic times one of the principal groups was the *candala,* which included members of more than one tribe. The *candalas* were required to live outside the villages. They also were required to make a loud sound whenever they entered the villages so that their presence could be known and they could be avoided by the caste Hindus. The *candalas* made their living chiefly by caring for corpses and by being public executioners. They wore the clothes of the dead, ate from broken vessels, and wore ornamentations only of iron.

The *panchamas* came about in other ways. In part they belonged to what has been called the criminal tribes, or castes, who made their living from unsanctioned activities. These were further subdivided into groups or subcastes that subsisted by theft and robbery, by fortune-telling and quackery, or by ritual killing. One such group, the Thugges, from whence comes the English word for thug, was a secret society whose members robbed and strangled their victims as a religious sacrifice to the goddess Bhavani, who is a form of the goddess Kali. The English in the last part of the nineteenth century were able to eliminate them by taking drastic measures, including open violence. As a result of these and other reasons, the *panchamas* constitute a very large sector of the Indian population.

The *panchamas* are lowly and despised. No part of the Hinduism of the caste system pertains to them. They are not eligible to study the Vedas or to engage in rituals; they are even denied the right to perform the *sraddha* rituals for the benefit of their ancestors. They are forbidden to live near the members of the accepted castes, and under no circumstances may they touch members of the four castes. They are, for practical purposes, regarded almost as subhuman and they live often on an essentially animal level. The constitution of democratic India, however, has forbidden any discrimination against the *panchamas* and indeed has taken measures to uplift them. But it must be said that socially derived distinctions are very slow to change even when they are annulled by formal documents and intentions. The Hindu scriptures speak of the *panchamas* as *avarna*, or casteless, and such many of them are even today. Nongovernmental efforts to modify the caste system, including that of the status of the *panchamas*, have characterized the modern period of Hinduism's development. The several reformers, mentioned previously, have made significant contributions. The westernization of India's life, including the travel and study of Indians abroad, also has been potent. These influences have made some headway, it is true, but there seems to be no well-founded set of reasons for supposing that the main features of the caste system will soon be eliminated. One of the chief influences for the maintenance of the system is Hinduism itself.

Ethics

A society is bound together by more than intellectual definitions of status. Generally a social system, such as caste, also requires an ethic. Ethical considerations derive from the junctures which individuals have with their fellow men. Ethics may also pertain to purely personal and subjective matters. But as the individual expresses what he holds to be a desirable relationship with others, he is in reality being a moral person. Some sense of ethics, then, it would seem, is essential to every man, although obviously there is no simple formulation which would satisfy all. The ways in which persons act in relation to others become routinized. An economy exists in not actually dealing with every situation as being absolutely unique. So, too, the ways in which persons act in relation to others become socially standardized. A society in concert with its members, singly and in groups, develops norms or patterns of acceptable behavior. These too may be called ethical. The caste arrangements in Hinduism and India's life, therefore, rest upon generally accepted notions of what is acceptable behavior.

It is remarkable to note that Hinduism, contrary to Western developments in philosophy, has never had a highly abstract and ratiocinated moral theory. Philosophical speculation in moral subjects does occur occasionally in the literature of Hinduism, such as in the dialogue between Krishna and Arjuna in the Bhagavad Gita. But there are few such instances in the whole sweep of Hindu literature. More commonly, the ethics of Hinduism derives from a variety of sources and situations. No unity, moreover, exists within these.

Hindu ethics in a major sense is derived from caste with its several supports. The caste system with its various taboos is also Hinduism's system of morality. The numerous and detailed prescriptions that regulate the daily life of the caste member define for him what his relations with others acceptably should be. The right ways of behaving are those which caste requires. No one requirement of proper conduct, moreover, is offered. The brahmin, for example, is required to study the Vedas and to shun alcohol. But the *sudra*, on the other hand, is not permitted to study the Vedas but is permitted to drink alcoholic drinks. Thus the requirements of the castes and the subcastes do not add up to a uniform set of social obligations.

The ethics of the caste system, moreover, is supported by other ideas within Hinduism's traditions. *Karma* is one such idea. *Karma* is in part the principle of moral causation. It signifies that every action is tied inevitably to consequence. No action goes unrewarded. Every act makes a permanently scored impression upon the character of the individual. There is no activity for human beings which does not count in the moral sphere, no accidents. *Karma*, moreover, is mainly linked to caste-required behavior. The requirements for conduct of the castes and subcastes, then, do not have social sanction alone for their support. That they have, but they also possess a more universal, permanent, and even

cosmic purport. The Hindu follows out his caste obligations because of essentially religious reasons. From this perspective Hindu
morality as expressed in the caste system is primarily based in
religion.

Another support for the ethics of the caste system is the idea of
the transmigration of souls. Death is not the end of things. The
atman is imperishable. Man is born and he dies, but he also is
born again. The consequences of human action, the result of
the operation of *karma,* are unending. What *karma* does not accomplish in this life will be secured in the next life or later ones.
Conversely, what one is in this life is a result of past actions.
The present life condition of the person is explainable by his past,
just as his future is being influenced by his present. Only by
breaking through the cycle of birth-death-rebirth and attaining
moksha (salvation) can one avoid *karma* and the transmigration
of souls. So the caste system with its socially stratified requirements for acceptable behavior is a foremost feature of Hindu
ethics.

In addition to the ethics of caste, however, Hinduism offers several other interpretations of desirable behavior. One of these has
been expressed in the four goals of life, as previously noted: *kama,*
or the pleasure-pain principle; *artha,* or the quest for power and
wealth; *dharma,* or the way of ethics and law; and *moksha,* or
salvation through spiritual knowledge and exercises. These constitute motives for living and may be said also to be a basis for
morality.

Hinduism also offers a long and varied list of *gunagunas* or vir-
tures and vices. These are qualities of conduct or dispositions of
character that the good man should practice or shun. The Upanishads, for example, provide such a listing: *ahimsa* (noninjury),
satya (truth-telling), *asteya* (not stealing), *brahmacharya* (sexual
continence), *maitri* (friendliness), *dharma* (fulfilling one's duty),
karuna (compassion), *virya* (fortitude), *dama* (self-restraint), and
saucha (purity). These virtues and vices are reduced to three in
one of the Upanishads. In this version, the gods, men, and demons

went on one occasion to Prajapati, who created them all, and asked him to tell them what the chief virtue was for them. Prajapati answered all three of them with a single syllable: *da.* The gods interpreted the answer as *dama,* or taming or self-control. The human beings thought the god meant *datta,* or giving or charity. The demons interpreted the response as *daya,* or mercy. Elsewhere in Hinduism's vast literature other listings of *gunaguna* are given. They vary greatly among themselves. Sometimes they seem to be directed toward rather specific actions, such as dietary require-ments; at other times they are more generalized, such as in advo-cating compassion.

Various categories of the *gunagunas* also are available. The Yoga philosophy, for example, places the *gunagunas* into two categories. *Yama,* the first, is related to the first steps in yogic practice and consists of various requirements of self-discipline and physical control: abstaining from violence, theft, greed, sensuality, and the lack of bodily discipline. *Niyama,* the second, is related to the second level of yogic practice and consists of divers internalized and spiritualized virtues that are required for the achievement of *moksha*: practicing charity, meditation, sacrificing, doing penance, studying the Vedas and other religious works, and remaining pure. In such a scheme the virtues and vices are obviously arranged in a pattern of ascension and worth. One step, or category, leads to the other. Taken together they form the basis for the fulfilled life.

Among the *gunagunas* the concept of *ahimsa* has held a special place. Many Hindus and others would claim that the doctrine of *ahimsa* (noninjury) is the supreme contribution of Hinduism's ethics. Positively stated, *ahimsa* reflects the view that all life is sacred and is to be protected and preserved. For some, *ahimsa* includes the plant world, thus creating practical problems as to human subsistence. For many, it surely includes the animal world. This means that no animal may be injured or killed. For many of these, therefore, a vegetarian diet is prescribed, although the prod-ucts of animals, such as milk, may be eaten. The precise way in which *ahimsa* may be applied for food purposes is often a subject of considerable debate and varied conclusions. Is a chicken's egg, for example, suitable for human consumption? The answer, broadly speaking, depends upon one's views regarding the nature of the egg, whether it has been fertilized or not. In the application of *ahimsa* to relations with human beings, the doctrine requires that one not harm in any way another human being. Harm in the form of physical violence, of course, is accepted as basic to the practice of *ahimsa*. But the idea also includes other forms of harm which may be mental and moral. In the fullest sense, *ahimsa* is a supreme ethical requirement, for by this one fundamental principle all of men's social relationships are governed.

Ahimsa, however, is basically a negative moral requirement or goal. It states what a person should not do; he should not harm any living thing. As such the principle in theory and in practice leads to a kind of moral neutrality in which positive acts of inter-human responsibility are not necessarily enjoined or required. Carried to its extreme, as it often is in Jainism, it leads to worldly withdrawal which is motivated by the fear that action may result in hurt to other living things. Asceticism, therefore, is one of the concomitants of *ahimsa* in its social practice.

In practice the concept of *ahimsa* has had significant consequences. Not only has it led to the widespread practice of vegetarianism in India, it also has been the driving force behind the monumental care for animals. Deriving from Jain and Buddhist times, Indians have built *pinjrapols,* or institutions, for cows, birds, dogs, cats, sheep, goats, and other animals. These are places where animals are fed and protected. If diseased or maimed, they are kept until they die. The pious Hindu is ready to share even the food that he needs for himself or for his family with needy creatures. At times it seems as though gross human wants are neglected in the interests of serving nonhuman but living beings.

Ahimsa, while a negative virtue, has been employed as a positive force. This paradoxical usage is most apparent in the life and teachings of Mohandas Karamchand Gandhi (A.D. 1868-1948). Gandhi took a precept which primarily had meaning within a highly religious context and deployed it within politics. He viewed *ahimsa* as a political weapon by which national aims, especially that of severance from the British empire, could be achieved. *Ahimsa* in this meaning became civil disobedience. It led to such actions as work stoppages, strikes, and other forms of noncooperation. When Gandhi's interpretation of *ahimsa* was accepted and practiced by the masses in India, it became a powerful example of positive force. The idea of *ahimsa,* also in modified forms, has been taken over by some American activists, such as Martin Luther King (A.D. 1929-1968), with or without a detailed understanding of the doctrine's origins and long history within the Indian experience.

Hinduism also is well aware of the fact that persons are not able to behave perfectly in relation to ethical norms and prescriptions. Sin is a reality in the teachings of the religion. The most general term for sin is *dosha,* although *papa* is also used synonymously with *dosha.* Sin in part is a consequence of the inheritance of past lives. The self has never been without limits and its course of birth-death-rebirth under the persisting influence of *karma* taints its basic nature. Simply to be born is to suffer from *sutaka,* or pollution. *Avidya,* or ignorance, also is man's lot. Ignorance means either lack of knowledge or actual error; both are a condition of all human existence.

In addition to the person's natural state as a result of *karma* and *avidya,* three other aspects of *dosha* are noted in Hindu thought. First, the person possesses and expresses a number of *vighnas,* or impediments. These may be considered the lesser forms of sin. Among them are those distractions that impede spiritual development: wealth, jewels, sloth, dancing, ill health, and betel-chewing. Second, the person also reflects certain *aparaddhi,* or guilty states of mind, that often lead to sinful actions: avarice, hatred, impatience, jealousy, self-righteousness, slandering, lust, gluttony, and pride These states of mind are more significant than the mere impediments, for they are the source of a variety of *papas.* They are more difficult to avoid because they are more subjective and pervasive within the human personality. Third, the person also engages in certain *patakas,* or clearly unethical actions. These may be brought about by reason of an overemphasis on some impediment. They more likely issue from a state of mind which without conscious control permits them to flourish. The *patakas* are classified into two categories. The lesser *patakas* are called *upa-patakas* and consist of such actions as the sale of a wife or child, usury, adultery, killing a person of low caste, teaching the Vedas for pay, and breaking an oath. The greater *patakas* are termed *maha-patakas.* These are usually five in number: the killing of a brahmin, willful abortion, drinking alcoholic beverages, stealing gold, and having sexual relations with the wife of one's guru. These *maha-patakas* are thought to be particularly venal and the person who commits one or more is said to suffer greatly in hell before being reborn again as an evil human being. *Dosha,* then, is a reality in Hinduism.

Hinduism as a complex religion holds complex views on the nature of the human community. It recognizes the necessity for government, especially in its monarchical form. Traditionally kingship has been the preferred form, although a greater degree of democracy exists in Indian villages than in the national life. Post-1947 India, however, has chosen democracy for its national life in a form which usually is called federalism. Carried also by religious tradition is the social system of caste and subcaste in which individuals have a socially defined status that is hereditary. Theoretically, and to a great degree practically, Indian society is not egalitarian; it is based upon a religiously sanctioned hierarchy of groups that are endogamously regulated. Hindu ethics, moreover, is largely a matter of caste requirements, although considerable but nonuniform provisions have been made for evaluating other facets of the moral life.

NINE

The Family

The family is the locus at which the person and society meets. Other loci exist, too, such as the person and the formal means of education or work or worship. All social institutions composed of individuals and regulated by particular functions that relate to human needs that are collectively realized are important junctures for the person. At various stages of personal development the individual goes forth into the community both to meet some of society's requirements of him and to challenge his needs for fulfillment. As a youth he enters the community to undergo the socializing experience of formal education. As an adult he goes forth into the community to utilize his knowledge and skill in some sort of productive work. In other ways the person is engaged in a serial and cumulative set of experiences by which his individual maturing is assisted and the ends of society are served. But the family is somewhat different. It is the social institution which surrounds the individual usually from birth to death. He may change from one family to another, from the family into which he was born into the family which he himself establishes and maintains. But commonly the person is a member of a family all his days. The family is the one and foremost agent of continuity for the person. He goes forth and back from his responsibilities and opportunities in the other social institutions. The home base from which going and returning takes place is the family. The family, moreover, is universally the most influential force for the person's character formation. This is true not only because of the amount of time that the individual spends within the family, but because of the nature of the influence. For it is the family's influence which is most intimate and persuasive. Here the bonds are of caring or love between the several members. Here, too, the responsibilities of transmitting family and general culture are most keen and practical. The family, therefore, is the chief point at which the person and society transect.

Hinduism has many important foci for its interests. A number of these already have been mentioned and briefly described. It also is strongly related to the family as the juncture between the person and society. Its teachings on the subject of the family also illuminate its teachings on the person and on society. The family is a primal bearer of the traditions of the religion. Indian life, both now and in the past, can scarcely be understood without some knowledge of the family and its related subjects.

Joint Family

The joint family has been the characteristic form of the family from the earliest times. The joint family has a number of features. It is agnate. That is, relations are traced through males on the father's side. It permits the possibility of adoption of persons into the family. The wives of male members of the family are also counted as family members; they leave their families to join the families of their husbands. The joint family also may include various other persons, such as unmarried daughters of some age, sisters, widows, an occasional uncle or nephew, and others. The various members of the joint family live together, usually comprising a very large household. They prepare their food in common and eat together. They hold in common a belief in traditional ways of relating to each other and participate together in Hindu worship. All nonmovable property also is held in common, although an obvious place is given to the propriety of personal possessions.

Further distinctions must be made regarding common property. Every joint family in India has a *kartri* (manager), usually the eldest male member of the family. He is the recognized head of the family in every way. But his authority is not absolute and it cannot be exercised in an arbitrary way. Concerning property, the *kartri* follows the requirements of a school of law. Of these there are two, named after the texts on which they are based: the Mitaksara and the Dayabhaga. Families in Assam and Bengal follow the Dayabhaga; in the rest of India the Mitaksara is the rule. In the Mitaksara school of family law, the *kartri* is in reality simply an estate manager. He has no right, for example, to give away assets so that his dependents will suffer economically. This school also permits sons and grandsons to take a share of the property even before the death of the *kartri*. In the Dayabhaga school the son must wait until the death of his father or the eldest male member of the family in order to share in the estate. The common property usually is divided among the sons at the appropriate time, for without this the size of the joint family would grow to an impossible size. Not everyone in the joint family has a right to the common property. Sons have a preeminent right; others, such as women and servants, do not share equally with sons. Sometimes the wife of the eldest male is given property rights after those of her sons.

The patrilineal and patriarchal family is the norm in Indian history. The eldest male member has duties beyond that of property management. He is the head of the family for all its functions. His will is decisive in most matters. But still he is not an autocrat in most instances. Legends exist which tell of the power of the head to sell or give away members of his family. These are legends that probably reflect either some practice or desire. In the main, however, the family head is a father in terms of his affectional bonds with the family members, a judge of sorts in relation to family disputes, and a bearer of Hindu traditions for young and old alike within the family. Like the executive of any large human enterprise, the family head has great potential for both good and evil.

Polygamy also has existed in India. The most common form has been polygyny, which is the situation in which a man has more than one wife. Despite the fact that monogamy was the rule, even in Vedic times the chiefs of tribes and the early kings were polyganous, as were the wealthier members of the various castes, including the brahmins. The primary basis for polygyny, in India as elsewhere, was the ability of the male to afford more than one wife. Hinduism, however, has not formally encouraged polygyny. The Apastamba Sutra, for example, clearly prohibits a man taking a second wife if his wife is of good character and has been able to provide him with sons. Other requirements also were laid down early, such as the one that required the husband to pay his wife an indemnity in the case that he took another wife. Yet the practice existed and Hindu tales abound in which kings and other heroes had dozens and even hundreds of wives, although at such a point the semantics of polygyny would appear to break down.

At various times in the past the women of a polygynous relationship were sequestered in the nature of harems. The Epics and the Arthasastra, for example, tell about these arrangements. The women lived in separate quarters, called *antahpuras* (inner areas). There they lived among themselves for the most part and were supervised by eunuchs, female servants, or old men. No one could enter the *antahpura* except the husband and those who served the women. In earlier times the harem women also were veiled. Some of the *antahpuras* were convenient and even elaborate places in which to live, but others were lacking in proper ventilation, facilities, and decorations. The husband, usually a king in past times, also had his obligations. At midday, for example, he was obligated to enter the *antahpura* to meet with his wives. He was generally limited to four queens and to them he had special obligations. They had sexual access to the husband by rule at least once each month. Otherwise the husband could choose among his other wives, although the actual choice often would be left to the chambermaid who officiated over the harem. The princes also had their own harems, but upon the death of their father the oldest son inherited his father's harem.

Another form of polygamy is polyandry, in which situation the wife has more than one husband; this form of marriage also has been known in various times and places in India. Although not widely practiced, polyandry was a family form in the earliest times. The Atharva Veda, for example, refers to this practice when it states that a woman may marry even after she already has taken ten husbands. Again, the Mahabharata tells how the five Pandava brothers had a common wife, Draupadi. Kunti, one of the wives of Pandu, the father of the Pandavas, also had several husbands and had a son even before she married Pandu. This arrangement among the Pandavas, however, was not looked upon as being in accord with the standards of the time and the traditional teachings regarding marriage. The relations between a wife and her husbands varied. Sometimes the wife married two or more brothers. At other times she married the male members of a whole family. The Mahabharata also relates that Jatila, the daughter of a Vedic sage, was married to seven brahmins. Various combinations, then, were possible. Even today polyandry is practiced among the Nairs, a generic term that includes a number of castes of Malabar, and among the Todas, a small tribe of herdsmen in the Nilgiri Hills of south India.

Matriarchy, while never dominant, also has existed in India. It indicates that women have played a significant role in the nation's life. Several legends of *strirajya*, or states ruled by women, exist in the literature of Hinduism. Quite possibly these point to actual situations in which women were rulers. In ancient times, moreover, queens often were the powers behind the thrones on many occasions, and in some instances in reality held authority. Among tribes of central Asian origin, such as the Sakas, Kushans, and Pahlavas, descent was traced through the female line. The Khasi of Assam is a matriarachy in which lineage is traced through the mother, she also being the holder of the common property and in other ways the genuine head of the family. The Nairs, previously mentioned, also trace descent through the mother. Among the Nairs, too, inheritance is transmitted through the daughters rather than the sons.

The eminence of women also is supported on religious grounds. In certain cases the female god is assumed to be more important than the male. The female deity is called *sakti* (energy) and those groups that worship the female principle are usually termed Sakta cults. Tantrism has made much of Sakta worship and a large literature has grown up which is devoted to this aspect of Hinduism, including the Saktagamas and the Tantras. Sakti is also the name of the consort of Siva, although she is also known as Parvati and Sati. She is worshiped as the ideal of sexuality and also of womanhood, possessing those attributes which Hindus most prize.

The joint family is in decline in India today. Admittedly it offers many advantages. It contains its own social security system. It is a basic social unit from which the caste system secures its force. It provides for a special kind of socialization process for the young. But it also has certain disadvantages. Its property system provides for more rigidity than modern conditions require. The rise of individualism as a basic cultural tenet in India, as in the West, also causes restiveness. The role of women, moreover, is not a happy one. The newly married woman, for instance, finds herself within an already established household in which she lives under the dominance of a mother-in-law and other women who have prior status. It is not unknown that some daughters-in-law are forbidden even to speak with their mothers-in-law by family-caste requirements.

Asramas

The course of the person's growth within the family bears further analysis. By tracing the stages by which the Hindu formally goes from childhood to old age and finally death, the panorama of Indian family life may be seen. Just as society was formally divided into four castes, so, too, the life of the individual ideally followed through four *asramas,* or stages. These stages are called formal for they were never realized in Hinduism's history on a mass basis. The *asramas* are not mentioned in the Vedas, although there are some references to them in the Upanishads. The orthodox later, however, taught that the four stages were essential to the religion. Probably they were honored in the breach. They do provide, however, a plan for human development in which a number of basic human needs may be met, and in this light they have been the subjects for wide discussion. They offer a convenient guide for an understanding of the Hindu family.

The first stage is the *brahmacharya,* or stage of religious living which broadly covers the period of adolescence. *Grihasthya,* the second stage, marks the life of the householder who is married. The third stage is called *vanaprasthya* and signifies that period in life when family duties have been discharged and the person retires to live in the forest. The last stage is that of the *sannyasa,* or renunciation, in which a person renounces all in order that he may devote himself to his own *moksha.* Each of these will be described briefly along with certain themes that are pertinent to them.

Children are the delight of the Hindu family and generally are well loved. Sons are especially prized and are desired also for religious reasons. They are desired, of course, to maintain the family name and, in earlier times, to assist in the defense of the family or tribe. But they have been important to the salvation of the father, for only a son properly can perform the rites of the funeral. The Sanskrit word for son, *putra,* which is of Dravidian origin, signifies that the son is a deliverer from hell. It was believed that without a son to officiate at the funeral a father would surely go to the hell called *Put.* Thus a newly married couple and their friends and relatives anxiously await the birth of a son, for a son is precious beyond words.

In fact, a number of family ceremonies are practiced that show the importance attached to child-bearing. One of these is the *garbhadhana,* which seeks to promote conception. Another is the *pumsavana,* which seeks the birth of a male child. A third is the *simantonnayana,* which seeks to ensure the safety of the child in the womb. At birth, before the umbilical cord is severed, the ceremony of *jatakarma* takes place at which *mantras* are spoken to the newborn child, a mixture of honey and *ghee* is placed in its mouth, and a name is given to the child which presumably is kept a secret until the child is initiated into the *brahmacharya* stage. The parents of the child are deemed to be ritually impure for ten days after the child's birth. After the ten days they are able to participate in their regular religious requirements and the child is given its public name. The early life of the child, moreover, continues under ritual obligation. Ceremonies abound and cover such events as the first feeding, the first feeding of meat, fish or rice at six months of age, the first cutting of the hair, *cudakarma* (which takes place in the third year and is restricted to sons), and the learning of the alphabet. While all these ceremonies are seldom practiced now, even by the more orthodox, their existence illustrates the importance attached to the child in Hinduism and especially the male child.

Sterility is an especially poignant problem to the pious Hindu. The woman who is unable to bear children is particularly despised and a man who does not have children from his wife is shamed. It is said that the gods do not hear her prayers; the husband has no one who will deliver him from the tortures of hell. In the past women who could not bear children were beaten and stoned, but more often they were returned to their own homes and the marriage annulled. In the past, too, various practices existed, such as impregnation by a priest, which today are not employed. The adoption of a son has been a major way of overcoming the disability of sterility or the inability of the parents to have a male child. If a man, for example, had married daughters who had sons, but he himself had no sons, he might then adopt one of the sons of his daughter as his own. If he had an illegitimate son, he could adopt him as legally his own. Even a widower or bachelor was able to adopt a son. Adoption is another ceremonial occasion, assuring the relationship in a public manner. Several forms of the ceremony are available; each depends upon the source of the male child and the nature of the relationship that is being affirmed.

The *brahmacharya* stage is initiated with the highly significant *upanayana,* or second-birth ceremony. This ceremony is performed for brahmin children at eight years of age, for *kshattriyas* at eleven, and for *vaisyas* at twelve. Children of the *sudra* caste and the offspring of *panchamas* were excluded from this great ceremony. The *brahmacharya* is the stage of the student, and *sudra* and *panchama* children were not permitted to study the Vedas. The rite of *upanayana* consists of a number of parts. The boy usually was dressed in the clothes of an ascetic. He carried a staff into the ceremony. The key to the rite was the placing of a sacred thread over his right shoulder. The material for this thread varied according to caste, but under no circumstances was he supposed to remove the thread for the rest of his life. Also, a verse from a hymn of the Rig Veda, called the Gayatri, was whispered into the ear of the boy by the officiating priest. Thus was he ushered into the first stage.

The *brahmacarin,* or one who has been initiated into the first stage, generally left his family to take up residence with his guru. The guru acted both as his religious teacher and as a substitute for the boy's father. The initiate was required not only to study diligently, but also to perform all requests of the guru faithfully, including some household duties. The *brahmacarin* mainly studied the Vedas, learning them through complicated systems of memori-

zation, including continuous recitation. He also tended the sacrificial fire and aided the guru in sacrifices. The formal period for
this stage was twelve years, although an especially pious *brahmacarin* could take instruction for as much as thirty-two years.
Theoretically the stage ended with the ceremony of *samavartana*
(graduation), at which time the youth was free to return to his
parents' home again. At graduation time the young man also
would take a *snana* (ceremonial bath), which signified that he
was immersed in his learning and his vows. After that he was
called a *snataka,* or one who has bathed. Finally, the *brahmacarin*
fed the sacrificial fires, embraced his guru's feet in homage, paid
the guru his due, bathed again and anointed his body, changed
his simple clothes, and left for home.

The *brahmacarin* was expected and required to be celibate. The
very term *brahmacarin* signifies celibacy. The Laws of Manu, for
example, describes sexual relations with the guru's wife as one of
the *maha-patakas,* or great sins, that required the young man to
do penance and generally leave the guru's household. A *brahmacarin* who has sexual relations with a person not of the guru's
household was required to offer a one-eyed ass to Nirriti at a
midnight ceremony. He also was required to wear the skin of the
ass and to beg for his food for seven days. The age at which sexual
stirrings were assumed to arise, between thirteen and sixteen,
involved the rite of *kesanta,* or the first shaving of the beard. This
was performed in the *asrama,* or house of the guru, and was accompanied by strong admonitions against sexual expression.

Not every one, even under ideal conditions, was able to leave
home and take up study within a guru's house. This was a luxury
that few could afford; also, the students were many and the
teachers were few. The *guru-kula,* or teacher's house system, had
to be supplemented by other means. The *charaka,* or wandering
teacher, also was available. Often the *charaka* was a young
brahmin who went about teaching young people for a fee which
he applied usually to his further study. The *charaka* tended to be
somewhat critical of the more established gurus and the formal

educational and religious requirements. Often they were the fore-runners of adapting the traditions to the changing conditions of Indian life and did much to keep Hinduism flexible through their liberal spirits. Various kinds of schools were established as centers for instruction not only in Vedic learning but also in secular sub-jects. The *pathasala*, for instance, was a kind of elementary school to which children were sent on a daily basis. The *tol* was an insti-tutional education system mainly devoted to Sanskrit learning. The Hindu temple often had a *matha* (cloister) attached to it in which instruction took place. The Saivite movement, moreover, had *akharas*, or facilities related to their monasteries that had educational functions. In addition, especially under the influence of Buddhism and Jainism, a variety of seats of learning that may be called universities were established, particularly in the medieval period. One of these was founded in northern Bengal by Ramapala, a Pala *raja*, in A.D. 1090 and was known as Jagaddala. It was a center for Tantrism and for the study of logic. The great university of Nalanda in Bihar was founded in conjunction with a Buddhist monastery and originally was a training center for Buddhist priests. Later, however, under the leadership of its abbot, Silabhadra, it extended its learning to include the Vedas, grammar, logic, the philosophies of Hinduism, and even medicine. Unfortunately, many of these universities were destroyed by the Muslim conquerors in the twelfth century A.D. But all of the persons and institutions of learning indicate that education has been a highly respected activ-ity within Hinduism and India's history.

The second stage of the *asramas* usually began when the *snataka* married. Marriage was assumed to be the obligation of every one, except those few who took vows of chastity and were devoted to a lifetime of religious study and practice. The term for the second stage is *grihasthya*, and it connotes the married householder. The *grihastha*, the term for the person in the stage, looked upon mar-riage as having three important functions. First, he was able to secure *rati* (sexual pleasure). Such pleasure was not looked down upon, but was assumed to be a highly legitimate goal of marriage.

Second, the *grihastha* expressed his maturity and responsibility for the maintenance of religious duties within the household. The family in its religious practices has always been deemed a significant bearer of the religious traditions. Third, the householder through marriage also sought for a son or sons by which his own welfare in the afterlife and that of his ancestors would be assured.

Both the groom and the bride ideally had to meet certain conditions. The groom was prohibited by the Vedas from marrying the daughter of his guru. He should not marry before his older brother was married, although exceptions could be made. He also should be potent and be free from a variety of physical defects. As for the bride, she should not be older than the groom; ideally it was thought that she should be only one-third the age of the groom. In the past, she should be married before her first menstruation, for this event was supposed to initiate her sexuality and if it were not met through marriage it would lead to various kinds of unacceptable behavior. She should not have been previously married; widows had special problems. Also, she should not marry until her older sister was married. In addition, she should meet certain physical requirements both for health and for beauty.

Both the groom and the bride are required to form an endogamous marriage, that is, they are expected to marry persons of the same caste. Endogamy is the caste restriction. There were times in the long history of Hinduism when such marriages were not universally practiced, although today, and from the time of the Muslim invasions especially, endogamy is the strict rule. Two other types of marriage have existed in the past and occur infrequently in the present. The one is the *pratiloma,* or counter-hair or against the grain kind of marriage. In it a woman marries a man of a lower caste. This form of marriage is condemned today as it was in the past. Persons who enter into such arrangements suffer in this life under the pressures of social sanctions. They also are said to suffer in the next life, being assigned to hell. The other form of marriage is the *anuloma,* or with the hair or grain kind of marriage. In it a woman marries a man of a higher caste. The *pratiloma,* or hypogamous marriage, is considered to be worse than an *anuloma,* or hypergamous marriage. *Anuloma* marriages were well known in Vedic and Epic times, but they have never been fully sanctioned. In fact, condemnations of it are to be found in several Hindu writings.

Until recently child marriage was practiced in India. It was supported by Hinduism. For example, the Brahma Purana says that a girl is eligible for marriage at any time after the age of four. The Ramayana states that Rama married Sita when she was six; he was sixteen. Usually the groom was much older than the bride, for he was theoretically obligated to complete the stage of the *brahmacharya.* Female children did not participate in the first stage. Many reasons have been given to explain the development of child marriage. It has been said that the female child was a handicap to the family, as women were generally viewed as inferior to men. Another suggestion is that Indian girls are more sexually permissive and that early marriage tends to place them under restraint. Also, the demand for virginity on the part of the man may encourage this practice. Other explanations have been offered. In some instances in the past singular variations in the normal practice have taken place. Thus, men of fifty or sixty years of age have married five- or six-year-old girls. This has meant that the girls most often outlive their husbands and are left in an especially demeaning state of widowhood for the rest of their lives. Again, the Mahabharata contains passages in which the marriageable age for girls is pressed to infancy and even to before birth. The existence of such teachings possibly reflects past practice on a small scale. Another variation is that of two children marrying. These may be betrothed to each other by pregnant women. The betrothal, however, may be broken, of course, if the unborn children turn out to be of the same sex. The Kumbi caste of Gujarat, moreover, has a marriage season of three days' duration which occurs only every twelve years. This caste insists on prepuberty marriage, so that on occasion girls in infancy are married. Child marriages still occur infrequently, although they were banned by the British in India in 1929. Officially marriages are restricted to males above eighteen years of age and females above fourteen. A number of Hindu reformers also led the way to the practical outlawing of child marriages.

Traditionally also a dowry is offered by the bride's parents to the groom. The Sanskrit texts refer to the dowry as *yautaka.* Evidence exists to suggest that in early times the traditional practice was reversed, that is, the groom's parents gave a dowry to the bride. This was a *sulka* (bride-price) and consisted of various forms of wealth, including the giving of cows. Gradually the practice became reversed to what it has been since at least medieval times. Hinduism has with some exceptions held women to be inferior in status to men and the dowry system is one indication. It both reflects and enforces the relationships between the sexes. It is one reason why parents often hate to have a female child, for such a child places a great economic burden upon them. Even the wealthiest families require this price for the marriage of their sons, and sometimes an inventory of goods that will be transferred is required in considerable detail, thus further demeaning the marital relationship. Once married, however, the groom must take full and final economic responsibility for his bride.

The composition of the marriage relationship is formally recognized according to certain types. These mainly reflect the situation in Vedic times, and today only a few of these forms are admitted. The highest form and the one most common today is known as *brahmya,* or brahmin-like. It connotes the marriage of a girl according to the acceptable ceremony to a man of the same caste with the giving of the dowry by the bride's family. This type of marriage, like the others, is based not only upon tradition but also on references to divinity. Thus the *brahmya* marriage reflects the successful marriages of Siva and Parvati and of Vasishtha and Arundhati. Seven other types of marriage also are acknowledged, although very few have survived. One is the *daiva* in which the girl is given by her parents to a priest as a personal gift or for payment of sacrificial services. *Arsha* is another form in which the father of the bride receives a pair of cows for sacrificial purposes. Another form is the *prajapatya* in which no dowry is expected or required. In the *paisacha* form, named after a savage tribe, the girl is raped and carried off by force against her will (while she is sleeping or is intoxicated, etc.). Similarly the *rakshasa* is marriage by capture, usually as a prize of battle. *Asura* is the name for the early form of marriage in which a bride-price or *sulka* was given. The final form is the *gandharva,* which comes close to the romantic version of marriage in which two persons deeply in love marry without regard to other considerations. One variation of this last type is the *saiva,* practiced among some Sakta cults, in which two persons are permitted to be married secretly for a short period of time.

The marriage ceremony in the Hindu tradition is long, complex, and beautiful. It is attended by many ceremonies both before and after the actual conjoining publicly of the couple. Each is prepared carefully for the marriage through a variety of ceremonies. The bride is helped by women who have borne a male child, but this does not include widows. Her body is anointed with powdered tumeric which is believed to increase sexual desire. Then she is bathed and her body is again covered with fragrant oils. Her face is decorated in various designs with several colors, and a yellow-dyed woolen thread is placed around her wrist by her mother. This thread is the *kautuka,* or nuptial bond, and is removed three days after the wedding. These and other activities prepare the bride. The groom undergoes a similarly detailed preparation. The marriage occasion takes place usually at the bride's house and the expense is borne by the bride's father. The actual ceremony may last for several hours and consists of the bride's father giving away his daughter, the groom plighting his troth with appropriate words as he holds the bride's hand, the couple's exchange of gifts, the bride's pledging that she will be a faithful and obedient spouse, circumambulation about the sacrificial fire, the sprinkling of the pair with holy water by a priest, and other ceremonial events. Following the marriage itself the couple then repair to the groom's household where for several days a number of other ceremonies are performed, including their looking together on the first evening at the north star as symbolizing their faithfulness to each other. Sometimes the marriage is not physically consummated until the fourth night or even until the tenth night so that evil forces within the home may be dissipated by that time. The couple, then, are fully ushered into the second stage, the *grihasthya,* or house-holder, stage.

As might be expected the home of the newly married couple is the center for many activities, but foremost among them, especially for the orthodox, is the conducting of the five daily sacrifices. By them the couple daily affirm their loyalty to their religion. Hinduism through family worship expresses a religious atmosphere which persists throughout the generations. The family is the support for popular religion. The five daily sacrifices are called the *mahayajna,* or great sacrifice; they also are termed the *pancha-mahayajna,* or the five great sacrifices, because it is believed that five types of beings are worshiped in them and that they include the five basic elements. First, the *deva-yajna* or deity worship may be performed in several ways. Originally it involved animal sacrifice, but today milk, curds, and butter may be poured onto the domestic fire or bits of sacred wood which have been sprinkled with *ghee.* Second, the *brahma-yajna,* or Brahman worship, consists of study, teaching, repeating, or meditating upon the Vedas. Dedicated to the sages, the sacrifice includes the recitation of the Gayatri Mantra, which consists of the first verse of each of the first three Vedas. When conditions preclude the conducting of the five sacrifices during the day, the Gayatri Mantra is repeated five times in the belief that it contains all of the ingredients of the *pancha-mahayajna.*

Third, the *pitri-yajna,* or ancestor worship, consists of *tarpana* (libations of water) and *pinda* (rice balls). These should be offered every day and comprise also a part of the *sraddha,* or obsequial rites, that are maintained for ancestors up to the seventh generation. Fourth, the *bhuta-yajna,* or spirit worship, takes place at noon to placate both good and evil spirits. Sometimes the good spirits are offered food on the ground, while food for the demons is placed in the garbage. This sacrifice also is believed to pertain to the animal world and, therefore, food may be given to both domestic and stray animals and birds. Fifth, *nara-yajna,* or man worship, consists of kindly deeds rendered to other human beings, especially those outside the family. It may take the form of extending hospitality to guests, of giving coins to beggars, and of feeding and otherwise aiding mendicants and others. These five daily sacrifices comprise an important part of Hinduism's popular appeal.

Once married, a Hindu couple are expected to stay married. Marriage theoretically is a bond uniting two persons in this life permanently and indeed for successive lives to come. The Hindu scriptures emphasized the indissolubility of the bond. An exception in the literature, however, occurs in Kautilya's Arthasastra, which sanctions divorce by mutual consent on the grounds of enmity. But commonly not even adultery has been a basis for divorce. For the man, adultery was a less serious offense, and the woman was required to bear her lot without complaint and certainly without recourse to divorce. Adultery on the part of a wife, however, was viewed more seriously and the wife could be punished in a number of cruel ways, including in past times the taking of her life by her husband. In practice the husband could divorce his wife for almost any reason through the rite of *nirakarana,* or expulsion. By this rite he simply renounced the marital relation. The wife was driven from her home and was not accepted by her original family. Usually she ended in prostitution. Since 1955, however, divorce has been legally recognized for the whole of India on a number of grounds, except that a man and wife who have lived together for twenty years or more are not permitted to divorce.

The final two *asramas,* or stages, in the life of the person are highly theoretical and are practiced indeed by very few. For the greatest number of persons the establishment of a family provides

responsibilities and opportunities which last throughout the lifetime. Only a few individuals would be able to go on to the third
and fourth stages. Only a few would wish to proceed. But ideally
the four stages provide for at least four major motivations in life,
even though they all may not be realized, and the third and fourth
asramas at least symbolically point to the requirements within
Hinduism of a fulfilled life.

The third stage is called *vanaprasthya,* or forest departure.
Hinduism recognizes that there is a time when ideally the responsibilities of the *grihastha* (married householder) are satisfied, when
children have been begotten and raised, the five daily sacrifices
faithfully performed for years, and duties to others and to the
community met. Then the maturing person leaves the family and,
alone or with others in groups, devotes himself to study and
sacrifices. He prepares himself for the final stage. Hindu traditions
differ on when a man should become a *vanaprastha.* Certain law-
givers say that fifty years of age is the acceptable time. Others
say that a man should retire to the forest when his skin becomes
wrinkled or he loses his sexual potency. Again, it is said that he
should wait until he has a grandson. Some even state that it is
possible for a man to take his wife with him, and others believe
that it is not necessary for him to leave his wife at all, but that he
may meet the requirements of this stage while still living at home.

Sannyasa, or renunciation, is the fourth and final stage of life.
In it a man renounces all his worldly possessions except a begging
bowl, a water pot, and his loincloth. He no longer is accountable
in a worldly sense, for he gives up all his familial and other personal associations. He is sustained bodily by begging. He avoids
human contacts entirely and remains insofar as it is possible apart
from other human beings. In avoiding human contact he also tries
to avoid speaking with others. In silence he is better able to con-
centrate on final matters. In fact, he no longer has certain religious
obligations. His entry into this stage may be marked by a ritual
burning of the Vedas. The instruments of sacrifice also may be

consumed in this final fire. Asceticism is the rule and *moksha* is the goal. He is preparing to die.

As a Hindu approaches death he is surrounded with ceremonies. It is believed that if a man dies in his bed he will be required to carry it into the next life, so at his final moments he is placed on the ground. Sometimes he is carried to a ghat and part of his body may be immersed in the water as an aid to his leaving. He may be placed among three fires and have *mantras* recited. Sometimes the leaves of a sacred plant may be put into his hand and *panchagavya,* or the five products of a cow, may be given him to ingest.

Following death the body is prepared for cremation. Cremation is the accepted way of disposing of bodies in India, although in early Vedic times the practice of burial in the ground was known. Traditionally a few special persons, such as infants, holy men, and yogis, may be buried. But cremation is the rule. Prior to cremation, however, a number of practices may be performed. A priest may recite *mantras* as a means of reviving the person and when unsuccessful may officially pronounce him dead. The body may be washed and invested with new clothes. The body may be carried to the *smasana* (cremation place) on a cart or on the shoulders of relatives. The procession includes mourners, sometimes professional mourners, who recite sacred verses and intone the names of the gods. Finally the eldest son walks around the funeral pyre three times, pouring a little sacred water on the deceased. Then he may break the earthen vessel on the corpse's head. The son then receives a torch which has been ceremonially lit. He applies it to the wood while the mourners chant *mantras* to aid the soul of the deceased to be released. It is assumed that a new body cannot be given to the deceased until his old body has been thoroughly consumed.

When the mourners return home they are obligated to bathe ceremonially so that they are purified. While reciting *mantras* they offer a libation of water and rekindle the family's sacrificial fire.

After a day or two the eldest son returns to the *smasana,* sprinkles the ashes with water, and takes the remains, which he buries or casts into a sacred river. Furthermore, by a number of rites the *preta,* or spirit, of the departed is aided in making the transition to becoming a *pitri,* or ancestor. By these ceremonies the *preta* is aided in securing a new body. Finally, another set of ceremonies are obligatory. These are called *sraddha* and are a form of ancestor homage. They vary from the more simple *pitri-yajna* of the five daily sacrifices to rather elaborate ceremonies involving many persons, including relatives, specially invited brahmins, and others.

The family, then, in Hinduism and in India's life is a highly significant social institution. It secures its meaningfulness within an essentially religious context in which all events and relationships are held to be relevant to the fulfillment of the religion's requirements. Ceremonies abound from the start of life to death. Throughout life the faithful Hindu is guided in his familial relations by traditions that have a religious sanction. The person views himself and others in terms of the perspectives and laws that tradition provides. The family, however, is not the complete and final goal of the individual's life. Some part of life ideally is appropriately devoted to the preparation for the next, including ascetic and renunciatory stages. Death, too, is not the end of life, but the transition into a new life under the requirements that faith has laid down.

Annotated Bibliography

Titles marked with an asterisk* are paperback editions.

Bouquet, Alan. *Hinduism*. New York: Longmans, Green and Company, 1950. A good, basic source.

de Bary, William Theodore. *Sources of Indian Tradition*.* New York: Columbia University Press, 1958. 2 vols. Copious materials that illustrate Indian thought since earliest times.

Fischer, Louis. *Gandhi: His Life and Message for the World*.* New York: Mentor Books, New American Library, 1954. The story of the Indian who led India's struggle for freedom and who taught and exemplified the teaching of nonviolence.

Forster, E. M. *The Hill of Devi*.* New York: Harvest Book, Harcourt Brace Jovanovich, 1953. The author of *A Passage to India* describes his life at court in the Indian state of Dewas Senior.

Hiriyanna, M. *The Essentials of Indian Philosophy*.* London: George Allen and Unwin, 1949. The best short introduction to Indian philosophy.

Hutton, J. H. *Caste in India: Its Nature, Function, and Origins.** New York: Oxford University Press, 1963. 4th edition. A comprehensive description from a long-term member of the Indian Civil Service.

Kublin, Hyman, editor. *India: Selected Readings.** Boston: Houghton Mifflin Company, 1968. A basic group of edited and annotated readings regarding the whole of modern India.

Macnicol, N., editor. *Hindu Scriptures.* New York: E. P. Dutton and Company, 1938. Hymns from the Rig Veda, five Upanishads, and the Bhagavad Gita.

Mahadevan, T. M. P. *Outlines of Hinduism.* Bombay: Chetana Limited, 1956. A valuable introduction to the study of Hinduism in its religious, philosophical, and ethical aspects.

Morgan, Kenneth, editor. *The Religion of the Hindus.* New York: Ronald Press, 1953. A comprehensive account of the nature, history, beliefs, and practices of Hinduism by practitioners of the faith.

Narayan, R. K. *Gods, Demons, and Others.** New York: Compass Books, Viking Press, 1964. Great tales from Indian myth and legend retold in English by a leading Indian novelist.

Nikhilananda, Swami. *Hinduism: Its Meaning for the Liberation of the Spirit.* New York: Harper & Row, 1958. A survey of Hindu beliefs and customs.

———, editor and translator. *The Upanishads.** New York: Harper Torchbook, Harper & Row, 1964. A faithful and graceful abridgment of the four volumes by the Swami.

Pitt, Malcolm. *Introducing Hinduism.** New York: Friendship Press, 1955. A sixty-page introduction to a complex subject.

Radhakrishnan, Sarvepalli. *Eastern Religions and Western Thought.** New York: Oxford University Press, 1959. Wise lectures on Hinduism and related matters.

———. *The Hindu View of Life.** New York: The Macmillan Company, 1962. A learned philosopher outlines the system of underlying beliefs that have guided ordinary Indian families for many centuries.

Renou, Louis. *The Nature of Hinduism,** translated by Patrick Evans. New York: Sun Book, Walker and Company, 1962. A brief, highly responsible introduction.

―――. *Religions of Ancient India.** New York: Schocken Books, 1968. A brief survey of the ancient sources of modern Hinduism.

―――, editor. *Hinduism.** New York: Washington Square Press, 1963. An introduction to both the history and the structure of Hinduism and a selection of classical and modern Hindu texts.

Sen, Ksita. *Hinduism.** Baltimore: Penguin Books, 1961. An exposition of the nature and historical development of Hinduism, with extracts from the Hindu scriptures.

Smith, Vincent. *The Oxford History of India,** edited by Percival Spear. New York: Oxford University Press, 1958. 3rd edition. A detailed and competent account of the whole sweep of Indian history.

Stroup, Herbert. *Four Religions of Asia: A Primer.* New York: Harper & Row, 1968. An introduction to the four religions that originated in India.

Wheeler, Mortimer. *Civilizations of the Indus Valley and Beyond.** New York: McGraw-Hill Book Company, 1966. A recent account of Indian antiquity.

Zaehner, R. C. *Hinduism.** New York: Oxford University Press, 1962. An apt introduction to Hinduism which concentrates upon the key concepts that underlie the changing surface of Hindu tradition.

Name Index

Subject Index and Glossary

72 73 74 75 10 9 8 7 6 5 4 3 2 1